PRACTICAL WAYS TO ENGAGE ALL STRUGGLING READERS

A Multi-Tiered Instructional Approach Using Hi-Lo Books

Claudia Rinaldi, PhD
Orla Higgins Averill, PhD

SADDLEBACK
EDUCATIONAL PUBLISHING

Y0-CAW-665

ISBN-13: 978-1-62250-892-1
ISBN-10: 1-62250-892-0
eBook: 978-1-63078-041-8

Printed and bound in India by Replika Press Pvt. Ltd.

18 17 16 15 14   1 2 3 4 5

Contents

Dedication

I would like to dedicate this book to my sons, Luke (11) and Samuel (7), who asked me often when I was going to be done because they wanted to read it!

—Claudia Rinaldi

To all the teachers and principals who have opened their schools and classrooms to us over the last 20 years so that we could learn alongside each of them. It has been an incredible journey to plant a seed of educational change and to come back and see amazing teacher engagement and student growth. You have given us ideas, inspiration, and hope that we can all work together to benefit all students despite language, culture, and disability!

—Orla Higgins Averill and Claudia Rinaldi

About the Authors

Claudia Rinaldi, PhD

 Claudia Rinaldi brings 20 years of experience to the field of education as a professor, educator, researcher, national trainer, and technical assistance provider in school districts. She currently serves as chair of the Department of Education at Lasell College in Newton, MA, known for their innovative online teacher preparation degree programs that concentrate on Universal Design for Learning (UDL) and school-wide multi-tiered systems of support (MTSS). Claudia focuses her work and research on the implementation of comprehensive school reform efforts using evidenced-based models including Response to Intervention (RTI), Positive Behavioral Intervention and Supports, and MTSS. In particular, her experience engages educators on how to improve systems and instructional practices for students with reading difficulties or disabilities and English language learners.

She serves as a board member of the Council for Exceptional Children, is a member of the advisory board for the Response to Intervention Action Network at the National Center of Learning Disabilities, and is a reviewer for the National Center on Response to Intervention and the National Center of Intensive Interventions.

Claudia is author and co-author of several publications on RTI, behavior disorders, learning disabilities, and issues related to English language learners, including "Response to Intervention for English Language Learners," "Response to Intervention: Educators' Perceptions of a Three-Year RTI Collaborative Reform Effort in an Urban Elementary School," and "Multi-Tiered Systems of Support (MTSS): The RTI and PBIS Approaches Involve Targeting Specific Areas in Which Students are Struggling."

Before joining Lasell College, Claudia was an assistant director at the Urban Special Educational Leadership Collaborative at Education Development Center, Inc.; assistant professor in the Teacher Education, Special Education,

Curriculum and Instruction program at Boston College; and before that, in the Department of Special Education at the University of Wisconsin-Whitewater. She received her PhD in learning disabilities and reading from the University of Miami (FL).

Orla Higgins Averill, PhD

Orla Higgins Averill brings 15 years of experience to the field of special education, with an emphasis on assessment and intervention, school and district leadership, policy implementation, systems change, and Universal Design for Learning (UDL). She presently works as a senior training and technical assistance associate with the Urban Special Education Leadership Collaborative. There she provides state- and district-level training, technical assistance, resource development, and systems and policy guidance to states and urban school districts across the country. She specializes in supporting the implementation of the multi-tiered system of support (MTSS) framework and has delivered training and technical assistance to hundreds of teachers and school leaders. Orla was trained as a school psychologist and is on the faculty of the School Psychology Program at the University of Massachusetts Boston.

Orla is a member of the Council for Exceptional Children, the National Association of School Psychologists, and the Massachusetts School Psychologists Association where she has previously served on the board. She is a proposal reviewer for the International Council for Children with Behavior Disorders conference and the co-author of numerous publications on MTSS and Response to Intervention (RTI). Prior to joining the Collaborative, Orla was a school psychologist in the Alexandria City (VA) Public Schools, the Quincy (MA) Public Schools, and at McLean Hospital. She received her PhD in curriculum and instruction from Boston College.

Introduction

When students don't learn the way we teach, let's teach the way they learn.

—Ignacio "Nacho" Estrada

In 2013 the National Assessment of Educational Progress (NAEP) reported that 33% of the fourth graders tested were reading at basic proficiency, with basic "denoting partial mastery of prerequisite knowledge and skills." Thirty-two percent of the fourth graders tested were reading below basic proficiency; these students struggle to understand what they read on a daily basis. In eighth grade, 22% of the students tested were reading below basic proficiency, and 42% were at basic proficiency.

We all have students who struggle. Many strategies and techniques have been developed over the years, but how can we use a coordinated approach to support all students in our classrooms: struggling learners, average students, gifted students, English learners, and students with disabilities? How can we leverage the best of research and the best of practice and make it work for the neediest students? How can we really engage students with content that draws them in and hooks them on learning?

As a teacher and a school psychologist, we have been where you are today. We have sat with students who struggle, and we have struggled ourselves. Why isn't anything working? Or is it? What can we do next? Should we do something different? How do we know what our students really need?

Let's begin by establishing some questions that we will address in this book:

- What is tiered instruction, and can it inform the way I teach?
- Is this something with a new name but not really a new solution?
- How can I develop a method that makes sense every year?
- How can I really differentiate for students in my class?
- How can I teach all the variety of learners in my classroom?
- What types of materials really work with all my students, and how can I use them effectively?

These are questions that most teachers have every year. These are also questions that many administrators hope teachers are in the process of answering as new students walk in their classrooms year after year.

What is new in this book? Can it really help? The purpose of this book is to provide teachers and administrators with feasible and effective strategies that can help all types of learners in your classrooms. It will provide you with the latest research-based methods that are creating change and improving student outcomes around the nation. We will present it in an understandable way that can easily be adopted in your classroom tomorrow.

Specifically, the goals of this book are to:

- introduce a multi-tiered instructional model for reading comprehension.
- integrate research-based strategies using hi-lo books for increasing reading fluency and comprehension skills of students who are struggling, are English learners, or have disabilities.

Let's begin with some common assumptions:

- We value all families and cultures.
- The first teachers are parents.
- All students can learn.
- All students don't learn the same way.

- All students can read and comprehend.

- All students should enjoy reading.

- As teachers we must strive to reach all learners.

- As teacher we must learn about each of the students in front of us each year.

- As teachers we value the strengths of each student.

- As teachers we are committed to figuring out what works for each of our students.

The following terms can help build a common language among those reading this book and can serve as an easy guide for looking back to definitions.

Struggling learners: students who have difficulty keeping up with classmates of the same age in a developmentally appropriate learning environment

English language learners: students who are not proficient in English

Students with disabilities: students who have been identified as needing special education services through an Individualized Education Plan

Research-based practices: instructional practices that are supported by research

Differentiated instruction: approach that recognizes that all students, including culturally and linguistically diverse students, are different and bring varying background knowledge, readiness, language, and interests to the classroom (Hall, 2002). As such, teachers must adjust—or differentiate—their curriculum and instruction for students who struggle and for students who excel.

Hi-lo books: high-interest, low-readability fiction and nonfiction books that appeal to struggling or reluctant readers

Universal Design for Learning: planning instruction proactively to both remove barriers to learning and to challenge and engage all types of learners in a typical classroom, including English language learners and students with disabilities

Chapter Summaries

In Chapter 1, we will introduce you to a framework called a multi-tiered system of support and its components, and we will describe how it and other initiatives in school districts work in concert with tiered instruction. You will learn how you can differentiate reading comprehension for a range of learners within this model using research-based strategies and innovative reading materials.

In Chapter 2, we describe how to use different types of data to learn about your students. We suggest that qualitative and quantitative data can help you develop an instructional approach that is effective and engaging. And we ask you to begin to think about profiles of struggling learners, English language learners, and students with special education needs. We also provide you with examples of instructional delivery models and a 90-minute reading block that is balanced and engaging.

In Chapter 3, we introduce and explain six reading strategies that you can use today to begin to improve your students' reading skills. We know that your classrooms are diverse and that you are challenged to meet the needs of your student population. You want a toolkit of strategies that are effective and feasible. But you also need strategies that can be used in a variety of formats, like pairs, small groups, and teacher- or paraprofessional-led groups.

In Chapter 4, we will examine individual case studies of students and look at what type of progress makes sense over time. We will provide you with questions to guide your instructional planning and intervention processes and described how hi-lo books can be used to support students' learning. We present how to monitor students' progress and make predictions about whether students will approach grade level or the end-of-year expected benchmark. Finally, we provide you with questions to consider if students are not on track, and how to know when to change an intervention approach to make it more effective.

Finally, in Chapter 5, we conclude this book by providing ways to monitor your own high-quality Tier 1 (core) instruction to ensure that it is differentiated, engaging, and balanced, and to ensure that it meets the needs of most students in your class.

CHAPTER 1

What Is a Multi-Tiered System of Support?

⬤A Look Inside the Classroom

Ms. Cuellar is a fifth grade teacher at an urban elementary school in the northeast U.S. She has been a regular education teacher for 4 years and has 24 students in her classroom this school year. According to school records and her observations, three-quarters of her students receive a free lunch and are low income.

The makeup of her class is 14 boys and 10 girls; 15 of the students are bilingual, with Spanish as their primary language at home. Some students in her class receive English as a second language (ESL) support and special education services during the school day. Her school district requires that schools use reading assessments 3 times per year. This school year Ms. Cuellar and her colleagues have been told that they will be implementing tiered instruction as the main intervention in reading and English language arts, but she is not sure how to implement tiered instruction. She also has not received professional development in this area.

Here are some questions that Ms. Cuellar and her colleagues have been discussing:

- How do I begin to focus on English language arts and reading instruction when I have so many subjects to teach?

- What is tiered instruction and intervention?

- What are interventions? And who does them?

- What does tiered instruction mean in reading?

- Are we going to get literacy materials? And will we get professional development so we know how to use the materials?

Tiered Instruction

Each year brings new students with unique needs. While these needs span the academic, social, and emotional spectrums, we know that the ability to read is the primary factor in determining future success. As you think about planning and instruction in your classroom, it is critical that you know how to ensure your students become better readers in measurable ways. One of the most research-based strategies to achieve this is tiered instruction.

Tiered instruction refers to a common practice in schools today that provides different levels of intensity of instruction. This includes classroom instruction along with additional instruction. In the past, additional instruction may have been reserved for tutoring sessions or given only to special education students. More recently, educators have begun looking at additional instruction as a timely intervention to prevent students from falling behind.

An intervention is instruction that supplements and intensifies classroom curriculum and instruction to meet student needs. It is provided to any student who demonstrates that they need more help to master a concept. An intervention can be academic or behavioral. All interventions must have (a) a plan for implementation, (b) evidenced-based pedagogy, (c) criteria for successful response, and (d) assessment to monitor progress.

Interventions have become part of a system of school change in the U.S. that is called Response to Intervention (RTI). Initially, many schools implemented RTI as a targeted program with intervention specialists pulling aside identified students to provide additional instruction. Now RTI has evolved into a multi-tiered system of support (MTSS). The most notable change with MTSS is that schools are encouraged to implement intervention instruction throughout the day in every classroom. If the school implements intervention instruction as a whole, resource allocation of personnel can be shared among the staff in more strategic and preventative ways.

A second aspect of MTSS is the focus on the whole child. In other words, teachers look at the context of the school, instruction, and academic and behavioral engagement when developing interventions. About 94% of schools across the U.S. are doing some aspect of MTSS (Spectrum K12 School Solutions, 2011). A cornerstone of this approach is collaboration among teachers to meet the needs of every student.

MTSS integrates research-based educational and psychological innovations from the last few decades to support students in more effective, preventive, and responsive ways, particularly in the area of reading development. Instead of waiting for kids to fail and then testing them for special education qualification, teachers provide them with supports as soon as they exhibit difficulty grasping a concept.

In this chapter, we will introduce you to MTSS and its components, and we will describe how MTSS and other initiatives in school districts (e.g., Universal Design for Learning, inclusion, and Common Core State Standards) work in concert with tiered instruction. You will learn how you can differentiate reading comprehension for a range of learners within this model using research-based strategies and innovative reading materials (e.g., high-interest, low-readability books; or simply, hi-lo books).

MTSS is a way for schools to organize how instruction and intervention can be delivered. Tiered instruction focuses on innovative instructional practices that have been shown to improve student achievement, especially in the area of reading. Joined together through an MTSS framework, these innovations are more powerful than if they were adopted independently in a classroom or even a group of classrooms in a school. The innovations that comprise MTSS include (a) teacher collaboration, (b) school-wide use of data to inform instruction, (c) inclusive instructional practices, including Universal Design for Learning, and (d) the Common Core State Standards, including standards-based assessment.

What Are Hi-Lo Books?

Hi-lo books offer struggling readers access to well-written and compelling fiction and nonfiction across all grades. These books present age-appropriate content—something that will grab a student's interest (i.e., high-interest)—at a readability level that is accessible (i.e., low-readability). Most hi-lo books appear no different from trade books, removing the stigma of "baby" books. Great hi-lo titles will give students what they need to become successful, independent readers. A great resource for hi-lo books is http://www.strugglinglearners.com.

Teacher Collaboration

Let's examine these innovations in more detail. *Teacher collaboration* refers to a practice where teachers with various levels of experience, expertise, and professional training address instruction and problem-solve how to remove barriers to learning in order to improve student outcomes in reading. This process happens during common planning time where groups of teachers come together to plan for individual students. The most effective collaborative sessions include all teachers and specialists who work with the selected students.

Data-Based Decision Making

Data-based decision making refers to the use of reading data, formal and informal, that is used in collaborative meetings to drive instructional planning for all students. Together, data-based decision making and teacher collaboration can result in a culture of shared responsibility for student achievement (Rinaldi, Higgins Averill, & Stuart, 2011). One type of data that this book will present is curriculum-based measurement.

Curriculum-based measures (CBM) are a key piece used in data-based decision making. CBMs are quick assessments that allow teachers to pinpoint students' basic reading skill levels. Knowing students' reading abilities allows teachers to better understand what students need to access grade-level curriculum, particularly in the content areas of social studies and science. CBMs are brief, valid, and reliable indicators of reading abilities needed to be successful at each particular grade level. Usually they are conducted in less than five minutes and are administered individually.

With CBMs, teachers can track the grade level students are reading at and how much they improve over the year. Using CBM results, teachers can document student progress and plan appropriate instruction and intervention. For example, in kindergarten, students must know the names of the letters of the alphabet and each unique sound, or phoneme, in order to become a successful reader. In seventh grade, students must be able to read accurately, fluently, and with inflection in order to be reading at grade level and have high reading comprehension skills. In both of these examples, there are CBMs that provide teachers with an indication of whether a student is at grade level and how much progress the student is making throughout the year.

Many schools administer CBMs to all students at the beginning of the school year to establish students' baselines. This allows teachers to quickly identify students reading significantly below grade level or students who are not English speakers. Tiered interventions can be established immediately for these students. CBMs can then be administered weekly or at given checkpoints during the school year. The frequency is up to an individual teacher or school. CBMs administered throughout the year allow teachers to monitor student progress and growth and make changes to intervention instruction as needed.

Inclusive Educational Practices

Inclusive educational practices occur when students with and without disabilities learn together in the regular education classroom with appropriate supports, planning, instruction, and curriculum materials. *Inclusive practices* refer to the ways educators address the needs of all students by determining their instructional levels and providing instruction at that level. In schools implementing inclusive practices, both regular and special education teachers receive professional development on differentiating curriculum and addressing the needs of students, with a particular focus on students with disabilities.

One very prominent way that inclusive practices occur in classrooms is through the use of Universal Design for Learning (UDL). UDL means planning instruction proactively to remove barriers to learning. UDL challenges and engages all types of learners in a typical classroom, including English language learners and students with disabilities.

UDL principles offer a blueprint that is flexible and customizable to meet the individual needs of each student using the "what," the "how," and the "why" of learning for planning and delivering instruction. These three principles help teachers plan instruction by addressing how curriculum will be presented to the wide level of students in a typical class, how evidence of learning can be demonstrated, and how engagement can be developed in order to increase student outcomes. For more information on UDL principles, visit the CAST website (http://www.cast.org).

Common Core State Standards

The Common Core State Standards (CCSS) provide a consistent expectation of what K–12 students should be learning in reading, English language arts, and mathematics. Although all states have had grade-level standards for education, the CCSS represents the first time the U.S. has published a common guide for establishing and assessing instructional goals.

Most states have adopted the CCSS and are transitioning from existing state standards and state assessments. One of the main goals of the CCSS is to provide a high-quality education for all students in the U.S. In reading and English language arts, the CCSS has defined the basic reading and critical thinking skills that students at each grade level should be able to perform in order to be college and career ready. The biggest change in English language arts is how the CCSS addresses the complexity of texts that students read, the type of texts that students should be reading, and the connection to writing.

In the area of basic skills, these standards are very similar to the state standards teachers are familiar with. Some of the standards dealing with complexity may be surprising. For example, in kindergarten, with prompting and support, students will compare and contrast adventures and experiences of characters in familiar stories. While in fifth grade, students are expected to independently and proficiently read and comprehend literature, including stories, drama, poetry, nonfiction, and graphic novels.

A Plan for Tiered Instruction

These innovations will be addressed in more depth in subsequent chapters. Each one will help you better teach your students to read and comprehend text. Keeping in mind that there are various definitions for these terms within the research community, this book provides general definitions and shows how these innovative practices are being integrated within MTSS.

As you read this, you may feel overwhelmed thinking about all of these innovations and how to make them work together in your classroom to meet the needs of all your students. All teachers face the challenge of helping students who struggle to learn. Some may be learning English as a second or third language. Some may have been identified as having special education needs. Some may have fallen through the cracks in earlier grades. How can you use these innovations to improve the academic achievement of all of these students?

Learning who your students are and what prevents them from accessing the grade-level curriculum is the key to success for everyone. As you plan your reading and English language arts instruction, knowing what interventions your students will need is essential in structuring time, space, and materials to help them. According to the National Association of State Directors of Special Education (Batsche et al, 2005) and others' statistics, approximately 15%–25% of students in today's classrooms will need some sort of supplemental support to access core grade-level curriculum and another 5%–15% will need intensive supports. It is important to note that if you are teaching in a high-poverty urban school district, this number may be higher. Many students will require intensive interventions.

Looking at your classroom through the lens of tiered instruction makes it easier to see that you will have students all along a continuum of needs. Using educational data to identify where each student falls on the continuum and to plan appropriate instruction is what this book is all about. As you read through the five chapters, you will learn how to plan for tiered instruction, how to pinpoint your students' basic reading skills the minute they walk into your classroom, and how to continuously monitor their progress so that you know when to use targeted curriculum materials (e.g., hi-lo books) that support reading outcomes.

Does this sound too good to be true? Perhaps. But the truth is that tiered instruction and intervention works for students of all backgrounds and skill levels. When you pay close attention to how you are implementing your curriculum and instruction, how your students are responding, and how you use the resources within your school and district, you can address the needs of all of your students.

The point is not to "wait for our students to fail." Instead, we must use the tools that tell us with a good degree of certainty which students are at risk. Then we must provide those students with the skills and practice they need to be successful.

➲A Look Inside the Classroom

Ms. Cuellar has 24 students in her fifth grade class in September. By October, she recognizes four students who are not making the progress that other students are. In an effort to help one particular student, Samuel, who is significantly below grade level, Ms. Cuellar refers him to the school's child study team. At the child study team, her colleagues—who do not know the curriculum she is teaching and may or may not know Samuel—suggest that she try several strategies. The meeting ends, and no one has told her how to implement any of the strategies. No one has said what to do, how often, for how long, how to know if it's working for Samuel, or when to make a decision about what to do next.

In other words, the meeting ends and there is no real action plan. There is no guidance to ensure that research-based interventions are implemented with fidelity. Nevertheless, Ms. Cuellar feels that the process was somewhat helpful and goes back to her classroom to try out one of the strategies, even though she's not quite sure what she should be doing. She tries the strategy for a couple of days one week and a couple of days the next week, but Samuel is still having a lot of difficulty reading. She is discouraged and refers Samuel for a special education evaluation.

As Samuel and Ms. Cuellar wait about 40 days for the evaluation to occur, he continues to sit in her classroom receiving instruction she knows is not working for him. During the special education evaluation, it is determined that Samuel does not meet eligibility. Ms. Cuellar is referred back to the school's child study team. Once again, the team provides her with limited information and supports on how to help Samuel. Ms. Cuellar goes back to her classroom feeling frustrated about the entire process.

Statistics on Reading Outcomes

- Research has found that children who did not read well by the end of third grade are four times less likely to graduate from high school on time than proficient readers. On top of this, a poor reader who lives in poverty is 13 times less likely to graduate on time (Hernandez, 2011).

- One-third of fourth graders in the U.S. failed to demonstrate even "partial mastery of prerequisite knowledge and skills" necessary to read and understand grade-level text as measured by the NAEP reading test (Denton, retrieved from the RTI Action Network, http://www.rtinetwork.org).

- For some groups of students, reading failure rates are higher than their same-age peers; 52% of African American students, 51% of Hispanic students, and 49% of students in poverty all scored below basic in the NAEP reading test (*Ten things you should know about reading.* Retrieved from http://www.readingrockets.org).

- Serious reading problems can be prevented when students in the primary grades are provided with quality classroom reading instruction along with additional small-group intervention when needed (Denton, retrieved from the RTI Action Network, http://www.rtinetwork.org).

Samuel's reading skills do not improve, and his grades reflect this. Two months have passed. Samuel is falling further behind.

You Are Not Alone

A tiered instructional approach can change Ms. Cuellar's challenge from one of frustration and discouragement to one of collaboration and continuous learning. Tiered instruction is based on the premise that students will need multiple levels, or tiers, of instruction (e.g., small-group instruction, additional time, specialized curriculum) as part of their system of support in schools. This means that schools expect that a certain percentage of students, generally 15%–25%, will need additional strategic supports, and that about 5%–15% of those already receiving strategic supports will need *additional* intensive supports.

Tier 1, Or Core Instruction

We can all agree that access to the regular core education curriculum (Tier 1) is vital for all students and that we understand that some will need additional or supplemental supports through an organized framework such as the one described here. And if the data indicates that a student needs more support, then that student will get additional intervention time in a second dose (Tier 2) or a third dose (Tier 3).

Why is Tier 1 so important? Tier 1, also known as core instruction, is the only time the students will receive the holistic richness of the curriculum aligned with the high expectations of the CCSS. This means that in Tier 1, or core reading instruction, teachers provide the basic skills needed to master the mechanics of reading (e.g., concepts about print, phonemic awareness, alphabetic knowledge, phonics and decoding, spelling, and fluency) and the knowledge-based skills to understand and draw meaning from text (e.g., concepts about the world, ability to understand and express complex themes, vocabulary, and oral language skills) (Lesaux, 2013).

⊃A Look Inside the Classroom

Remember Ms. Cuellar's frustration? Let's look at how intervention can work with an MTSS approach.

Ms. Cuellar has 24 students in her fifth grade class in September. Her universal screening assessments have indicated that four students are not responding to the instruction and intervention. She begins to monitor their progress using CBMs. They are not making the progress other students are.

At her weekly grade-level meeting, Ms. Cuellar and her colleagues discuss these four students, including Samuel. Ms. Cuellar brings Samuel's universal screening reading data taken in September plus the progress monitoring data from October to the meeting. Because these meetings have a structured protocol that guides collaborative problem-solving and discussion, Ms. Cuellar knows that she will present the progress monitoring data points and will also share information from a diagnostic reading comprehension test she administered. She knows her colleagues, who are teaching the same grade-level curriculum, will partner with her in finding an instructional approach that works for Samuel.

At the meeting, she summarizes that Samuel scored on the low range of decoding skills. The universal screener and progress monitoring tool also showed poor reading fluency when compared to students in his grade at this time of the year. Ms. Whitney, another fifth grade team member, offers to bring Samuel to the school's intervention block, called "SUCCESS time," for 20 minutes, 3 times per week for 6 weeks. During SUCCESS time, Ms. Whitney is working with a small group of four students on decoding and fluency with hi-lo books. All of the students in the intervention block are at the same instructional reading level as Samuel.

The team documents their planning conversation and summarizes the intended intervention delivery sessions for the next 6 weeks. They decide to review Samuel's progress in 6 weeks and determine the specific follow-up date, which they put on the calendar. During this meeting, the grade-level team collaborates to review data, discuss curriculum and instruction, and develop a measurable action plan with a clear progress monitoring schedule to improve Samuel's reading that leverages the supports that the school has implemented (i.e., the intervention block).

The MTSS Framework in Action

As discussed, MTSS is an approach to prevention and intervention that uses instructional data to guide problem solving and planning within a tiered system of support. This approach, based on research, expects that 75%–80% of students will benefit and respond to a strong Tier 1 (core) reading curriculum using the CCSS as a basis for a high-quality education (Batsche et al, 2005; Pavri, 2010).

Teachers collaborate to address any barriers to the implementation of Tier 1 (core) instruction until most of the students are benefitting. The framework also expects that 15%–25% of students will need *additional* strategic short-term intervention, called Tier 2 (Batsche et al, 2005; Marston, 2005; Pavri, 2010). This short-term intervention focuses on the area of deficit in basic reading skills (i.e., phonemic awareness, phonics, fluency, comprehension, and vocabulary). Tier 2 occurs in 20-minute segments, 3 times per week for 12–17 weeks. The goal of this Tier 2 intervention is to increase the number of students responding or benefitting from Tier 1 (core) instruction.

The framework also addresses the remaining 5%–15% of students who will need intensive intervention in addition to Tier 1 (core) and Tier 2. This *additional* intensive intervention, known as Tier 3, is delivered in a smaller teacher–student ratio of 1:1 or 1:3 for at least 50 minutes, 3 times per week, with progress monitoring occurring weekly. The goal here is to ensure that students are getting exposure to Tier 1 (core), Tier 2, and Tier 3 supports anytime they are needed.

Figure 1 is a graphic that represents the MTSS framework in reading and how it addresses the main components of tiered instruction: assessment, instruction, and intervention. This example also provides a practical application that identifies how materials can be used within each tier of support.

In looking at Figure 1, you see that the triangle represents all students receiving Tier 1 (core) instruction within a differentiated instructional approach using the principles of UDL and the expectations of the CCSS. You also see how differentiated instructional materials, like hi-lo books and emergent readers, can support Tier 1 (core) instruction at the Tier 2 level of support.

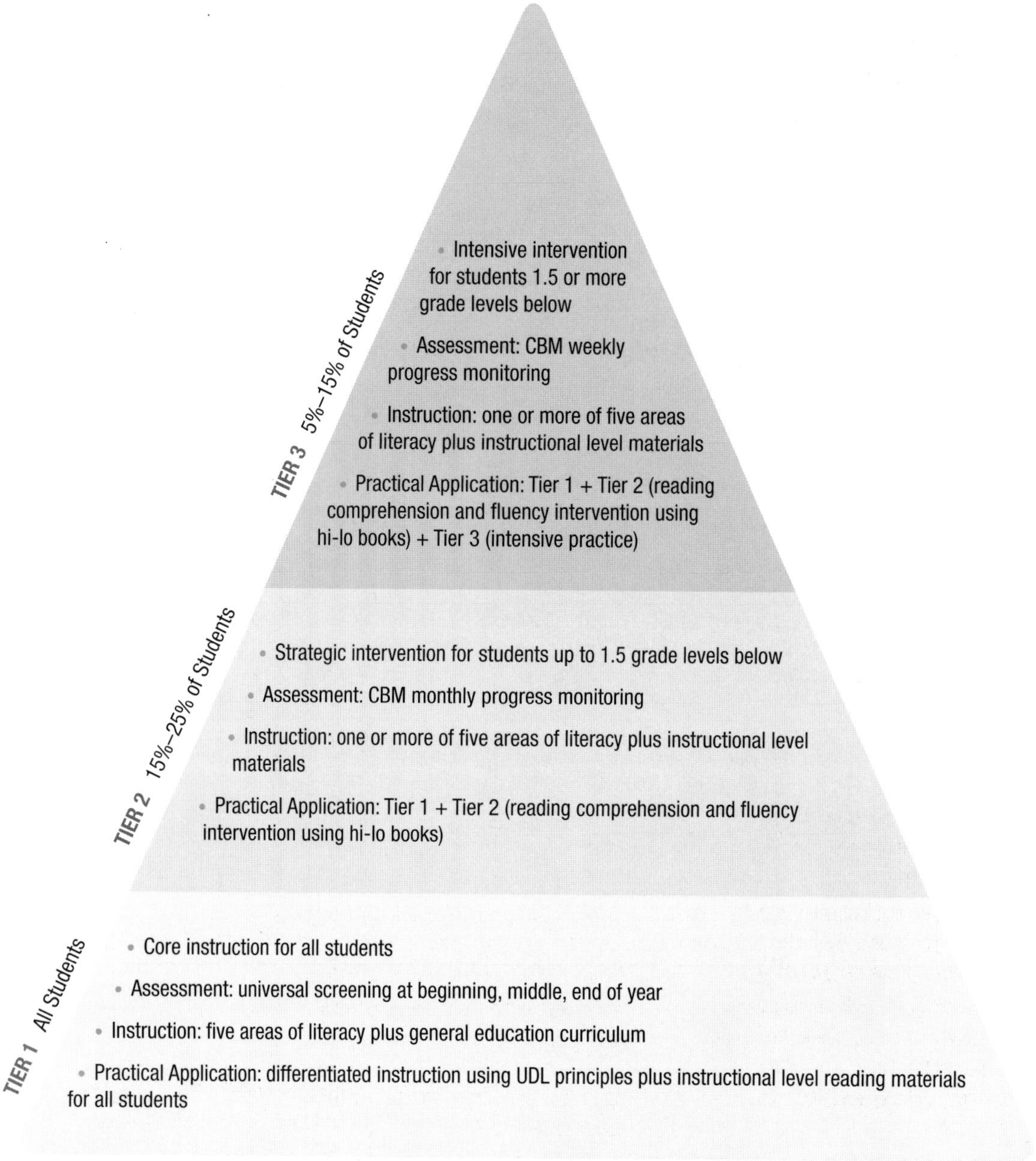

Tier 3 5%–15% of Students

- Intensive intervention for students 1.5 or more grade levels below
- Assessment: CBM weekly progress monitoring
- Instruction: one or more of five areas of literacy plus instructional level materials
- Practical Application: Tier 1 + Tier 2 (reading comprehension and fluency intervention using hi-lo books) + Tier 3 (intensive practice)

Tier 2 15%–25% of Students

- Strategic intervention for students up to 1.5 grade levels below
- Assessment: CBM monthly progress monitoring
- Instruction: one or more of five areas of literacy plus instructional level materials
- Practical Application: Tier 1 + Tier 2 (reading comprehension and fluency intervention using hi-lo books)

Tier 1 All Students

- Core instruction for all students
- Assessment: universal screening at beginning, middle, end of year
- Instruction: five areas of literacy plus general education curriculum
- Practical Application: differentiated instruction using UDL principles plus instructional level reading materials for all students

FIGURE 1 The MTSS Framework in Reading and Language Arts

In Tier 2, the instructional intervention responds to the identified area of reading difficulty and the instructional level of the students. Students meet in small groups and receive direct instruction of skills, immediate corrective feedback, and the opportunity to develop critical thinking skills in a strategic and targeted way. As this intervention is delivered, there is a clear action plan that outlines frequency of delivery (e.g., 20 minutes, 3 times per week), a schedule to monitor progress (e.g., monthly fluency probes using CBM), and instructional materials (e.g., hi-lo books) that can change as the student makes progress in the instructional level.

In Tier 3, the frequency of the instructional intervention is increased (e.g., 50 minutes, 3 times per week), and the intensity of delivery is increased.

What Is Differentiated Instruction?

Although a strong reading curriculum will provide the foundation for effective instruction, teachers cannot simply follow the script from the teacher's manual. Doing so would neglect the unique needs of all students. Teachers need to adjust, or *differentiate*, their curriculum and instruction for students who struggle and for students who excel.

Differentiated instruction recognizes the ability of students at or below grade level and assumes that all students, including culturally and linguistically diverse students, are different and bring varying background knowledge, readiness, language, and interests to the classroom (Hall, 2002). Teachers can differentiate Tier 1 (core), Tier 2, and Tier 3 reading instruction for students who struggle by:

- using assessment data to inform the scope and sequence of the specific skills and strategies being taught.

- providing explicit instruction that includes modeling of skills and strategies and offers clear descriptions of new concepts.

- providing opportunities for independent practice with a variety of instructional materials that increase confidence, comfort, and skill level (e.g., using hi-lo books).

- increasing opportunities for practice in flexible groupings with teachers and peers.

- providing a balance between teacher-selected and student-selected tasks and assignments—giving students choices in their learning.

- providing "just-right," engaging texts at students' instructional reading levels (e.g., hi-lo books).

- providing corrective feedback that calls clear attention to student mistakes and offers student opportunities to try again.

- varying expectations and requirements for students' responses by allowing for varied means of expression, alternative procedures for completion, and varying degrees of difficulty.

- monitoring students' understanding of key skills and strategies and re-teaching when necessary.

A Look Inside the Classroom

In the case of Ms. Cuellar, the RTI framework guarantees that Samuel will receive targeted intensive instruction *in addition* to the rich and differentiated curriculum he receives in Tier 1. Because all decisions about instruction are informed by data, Ms. Cuellar feels relieved to know that if after 6–8 weeks the data indicates that Samuel is not responding to his Tier 2 intervention, the action plan will be adjusted. Further, Ms. Cuellar will not be alone in trying to figure out how to support Samuel as the year continues. Because the MTSS model includes regular structures for collaborative problem solving, Ms. Cuellar and her grade-level team members will share responsibility for Samuel's achievement. Together they will develop a plan that responds to his areas of need.

Finally, let's not forget that Ms. Cuellar has 23 other students, some of whom are English language learners, some of whom struggle like Samuel, some of whom already receive special education services, and some of whom are performing well above the fifth grade level. The MTSS framework guarantees that all of these different learners will participate in a rich and differentiated Tier 1 (core) curriculum. When assessment data indicates that some of these students may need more strategic or intensive support, the collaborative problem-solving structure enables teachers to share expertise and develop clear action plans for the delivery of Tier 2 or Tier 3 interventions that respond to each student's unique challenges.

Summary

In this chapter, we introduced you to a framework to address instruction called MTSS. We described how many innovations and current instructional practices fit within the model and can be integrated to provide more effective instructional support to students who are struggling, who are second language learners, or who have a disability. We began to explain how schools can capitalize on and refine existing structures to develop practices that enable teachers to carry out strong and responsive reading instruction. These structures include collaboration, data-based decision making, inclusive practices, and CCSS.

By now you should be starting to develop an understanding of the basic features of MTSS, but you may still be feeling a little overwhelmed. How do you provide tiered instruction effectively? What does it actually look like in a classroom? In upcoming chapters, we will provide more detail about how this actually works in the classroom.

You will learn more about Ms. Cuellar, her colleagues, her student Samuel, and other students in her class. We will provide you with more detailed information on how to teach reading more effectively using research-based practices. We will offer examples of how curriculum and instructional materials are used effectively to support diverse learners in your classrooms. Whether your school has MTSS in place or not, tiered instruction will help you address the needs of all your students.

CHAPTER 2

How Can I Teach the Variety of Learners in My Classroom?

⮌A Look Inside the Classroom

We were introduced to Ms. Cuellar and her student Samuel in the last chapter. In this chapter, we are going to see how Ms. Cuellar begins to look at student data. How she uses the data to plan for effective instructional delivery. Which instructional practices she can use to teach students where they are. How she can select materials based on the individual needs of students (e.g., hi-lo books). And how she can be assured that every student is making progress.

Ms. Cuellar has 24 students in her fifth grade class. As she begins to plan how to teach reading to her students, she starts by looking at who her students are. Although she has met them and sees them every day, she really has not had a chance to understand who they are as learners in her classroom. To do that, Ms. Cuellar looks at different sources of data to be able to plan for instruction. She will find out as much as she can about each of her students so that she will be better able to plan for reading instruction.

Why Should I Learn More About My Students?

Learning about each of the students in your class is very important as you begin to plan for instruction. Long ago, teachers used lesson plans that they did year after year, or a new teacher used lesson plans they developed in college. This style of teaching does not meet the needs of today's classrooms. As the country's population changes, schools look very different across urban, suburban, and rural settings. Educators must be culturally responsive to the students who come to them each year.

Research tells us that in order for our lessons to be culturally responsive, teachers must learn about the background of the students in front of them. Teachers must use this information when developing the lesson plans. And they must deliver differentiated instruction that will result in student success.

Do you remember sitting in a classroom when you were a student in grade school and not really understanding a concept the teacher taught? What did the teacher do? He or she probably went on and hoped that most of the class got the concept so that he or she could move on to the next concept. Teaching this way—"hope and move on"—does not meet the needs of all students and leads to failure for those students who never catch up. With today's teacher evaluation systems using student growth and state assessment outcomes as criteria for teacher effectiveness, our approach to lesson planning has to change. This is what tiered instruction is all about.

You may ask why we have not adjusted instruction before. In the last two decades, we have learned a lot about differentiating instruction to teach students who are above grade level, at grade level, just below grade level, and significantly below grade level. We also know that we cannot let students pass without successfully learning the standards and skills to be career and college ready. Given how important literacy is for a successful life, we also know that whether teachers are certified to teach math, English, or science, they are also teachers of reading. Therefore, it is critical to use data to set up the right conditions for teaching, learning, and students' success.

Qualitative Data Is Virtually Any Information That Is Not Numerical in Nature.

"Data" is the information you know about your students. What kind of data do you have when it comes to your students? You may notice that some of your students are very social and like to chat with their friends, even during direct instruction. You may notice that others are interested in music and would prefer to listen to it through their headphones rather than engage in collaborative learning. Some students prefer math over social studies. Some students like working on the computer, and others like doing group work. One of your students is always talking about her soccer games and how much she loves watching soccer with her cousins. These observations are all forms of qualitative data that help you plan how you will teach and reach each of your students. With this qualitative data you may, for example, incorporate activities that involve music or technology or group work.

What Do I Already Know About My Students? What Does Data Tell Me About Them and Their Reading Skills?

Effective instruction is a skill that teachers develop over time, but we know that the capacity to deliver high-quality instruction hinges on what teachers know about the students they are instructing. In Chapter 1, we identified "data-based decision making" as one of the innovations that comprise MTSS.

It is a critical component of any research-based instructional strategy.

Together, qualitative and quantitative data help you differentiate your instruction to better meet the needs of all learners in your classroom. Figure 2 shows Ms. Cuellar all the available data she has on her student Samuel. Let's think about how you can learn about the cultural backgrounds of your students, as well as their individual strengths and weaknesses, to create a learning profile for each student.

Figure 3 illustrates how you can begin your data collection in the "Getting to Know You Information Form." This form lets you see how your students identify themselves personally and academically. It provides you with information on how insightful they are regarding their own learning styles, and it allows you to gauge their interest in school and in reading.

Quantitative Data Is Information That Can Be Counted or Expressed Numerically.

You likely also gather a lot of quantitative data (e.g., grades, state test scores, CBM, end of chapter tests, quizzes) about your students. Quantitative data includes information like a student's scores on quizzes and state assessments. It also includes how many times a student has been absent from or tardy to school, or how many times a student has asked to visit the school nurse. Like qualitative data, quantitative data helps you make adjustments to instruction. For example, if several students miss the same prediction-related questions on a comprehension test, you may want to re-teach the prediction strategy to that group of students. If a student is asking to see the nurse every day during English language arts, he or she may be avoiding reading or writing and may require extra help or strategies more suited to his or her learning strengths.

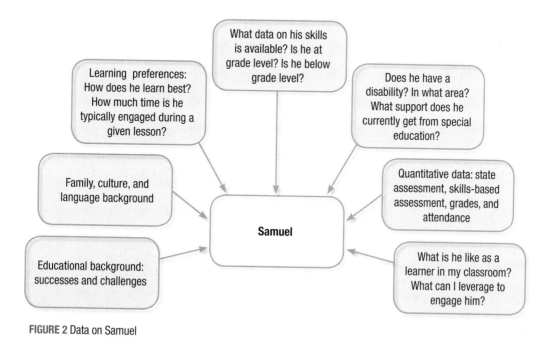

FIGURE 2 Data on Samuel

"Getting to Know You" Information Form

NAME: _____ DATE: _____

Directions: All about you! Fill out the form. Write as much about yourself as you can.

Draw a picture of yourself or something that represents who you are.	What language other than English do you speak? _____ What language would you like to learn to speak? _____ What is your favorite thing to do after school? _____ _____ _____ _____
What do you like best about school? _____	Do you have siblings? Younger or older? _____
If you could change one thing about school, what would it be? _____ _____ _____ _____	How do you do your homework? ☐ In silence at a desk ☐ In silence somewhere else ☐ With music at a desk ☐ With music in your room ☐ With many breaks ☐ Quickly, no breaks
What activities in class help you learn best? _____	What is your favorite subject? _____
Describe the things your favorite teacher did when he or she was teaching? _____	What is the most difficult thing you have been asked to do in school? _____
What activities do you like to do in class from most to least, using 1 as the most and 5 the least. _____ Listen to the teacher _____ Engage in class discussion _____ Work in small groups _____ Work in pairs _____ Work on the computer _____ Present your work in front of the class _____ Debate ideas with other students	Check the types of books you are familiar with. ☐ Graphic novels ☐ Classics ☐ E-books ☐ Fiction ☐ Nonfiction

FIGURE 3 "Getting to Know You" Information Form

This is a form of qualitative data that allows you to select from a variety of hi-lo books according to your students' interests and at their independent and instructional reading levels.

Once you have basic information about your students, it is critical to continue to gather other sources of educational data. But from where? Look at the official education records that are available for every student in the school office. In these educational records, you will see that there is a lot of qualitative and quantitative data. You can learn about your students' educational backgrounds. A disruption. A repeated grade. Bilingual. Multilingual. Grades and state assessment results from the previous year. You can also learn if your students have been referred to special education, if they were eligible for services, what the area(s) of disability are, and what type of services (e.g., specialized instruction by the special education teacher, occupational therapy, speech and language services) you need to have in place.

Let's review some of the interpretations you can make from these types of records. One source of data is information on whether a student has repeated a grade. If so, the school and parent(s) have agreed to this, and it will have been documented. Repeating a grade is a good indicator that the student has been a struggling learner.

Other quantitative sources of information in the educational records include grades, work samples, and district-based reading assessments. Scores on the state assessment are also a very good source of information. State assessments usually include percentile scores that are based on the bell curve as in Figure 4. Percentile scores are distributed across 100 percentage points according to the bell curve's breakdown between below average

Categories of Disability Under IDEA

- Autism
- Deaf-blindness
- Deafness
- Developmental delay
- Emotional disturbance
- Hearing impairment
- Intellectual disability
- Multiple disabilities
- Orthopedic impairment
- Other health impairment
- Specific learning disability
- Speech or language impairment
- Traumatic brain injury
- Visual impairment, including blindness

to average to above average. This score helps educators know which students may have difficulty when compared to all the students who took the test. Any score above the 15th percentile means that the student is performing at least within average limits. Average suggests that students should be able to learn and perform grade-level curriculum unless there is a disability. While this one score can't provide us with a complete picture, it works with other data sources to help build the profile of each of your students.

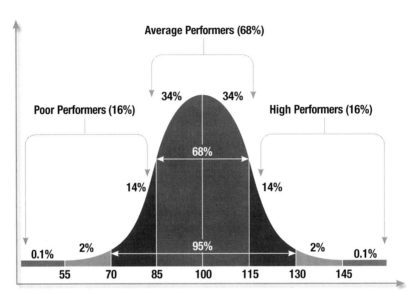

FIGURE 4 Bell Curve Percentile Scores

To start with this data source, ask your principal for the state assessment results. Create and fill out a "State Assessment Class-Wide View Form" like the one in Figure 5.

Student's Name	Above 84th Percentile	15th–83rd Percentile	2nd–14th Percentile	< 2nd Percentile
1. Samuel			X	
2.				
3.				
4.				
5.				

FIGURE 5 State Assessment Class-Wide View Form

Take a look and notice which of your students is below the 15th percentile and which is below the 2nd percentile. Any score below the 2nd percentile would indicate a particularly significant skill deficit. Also note which students score well above average (i.e., receive scores above the 84th percentile). Ms. Cuellar has noted Samuel's score between the 2nd and 14th percentile.

District Assessments

Now that you know how your students perform in the state assessments, you can also look at other assessments that your district has. Two examples that are very common in schools are the Dynamic Indicators of Basic Early Literacy Skills (DIBELS) and AIMSweb (up to Grade 8). Both data management systems work with districts across all 50 states. These assessments are CBMs because they allow educators to know what basic reading skills a student may have at any point during the year, and how quickly the student is gaining toward end-of-year skills in reading for that grade. These assessments have looked at content written at each grade level from many curriculum materials and broken it down by the length of sentences, complexity of the sentences, vocabulary, decoding ability, and comprehension levels.

Standardized tests have been given to thousands of students to provide teachers with the expected average rates of reading, or benchmark scores, at the beginning, middle, and end of a given grade from kindergarten through eighth grade. Teachers can compare how their students are actually reading with how they are expected to be reading. This gives another data point with which to make instructional decisions. The CBM is best described as the ability to read orally, both fluently and accurately, given a grade-level text sample. Specifically, the CBM is administered to individual students by providing them with a reading selection at grade level. The student is provided with a 1-minute time period to read the text while the teacher tracks the number of words read correctly and summarizes the strategies the students use as they read. This CBM is a highly effective indicator of the growth of reading skills. Teachers can use it at any time with any student to get a baseline, track progress over time, or summarize at the end of the year.

CBMs are also very effective for students with major reading challenges because teachers can use reading selections from hi-lo books at the students' reading level and track progress using those in addition to grade-level text. The benefit is that although a student in fifth grade reading at an equivalent to second grade reading level will always look like he or she is failing grade-level materials, he or she may be showing great progress moving from second grade hi-lo books to third or even fourth grade hi-lo books. CBMs are very sensitive to student growth, and there are recommended tables available to let you know how the student is improving.

Figure 6 is an adapted version by Hasbrouck and Tindal (2006) Oral Reading Fluency Norms used for grade-specific CBM in oral reading fluency. Note each number is minimal for accessing curriculum materials at grade level. The goal should be to surpass these numbers.

Grade	Fall Norms WCPM	Winter Norms WCPM	Spring Norms WCPM
1		12	28
2	25	42	61
3	44	62	78
4	68	87	98
5	85	99	109
6	98	111	122
7	102	109	123
8	106	115	124

WCPM = words correct per minute. Please note that if your school is using a district-wide assessment like DIBELS or AIMSweb, the numbers may be slightly different. The scores are based on Hasbrouck and Tindal (2006) 25th percentile rank norm and should be used as a minimum standard for accessing grade-level text.

FIGURE 6 Who Needs Fluency Instruction?

⮕A Look Inside the Classroom

Let's look at what Ms. Cuellar now knows about some of her students using Figure 7's fifth grade CBM oral reading fluency score.

Student	Expected Score Beginning of Year > 85 WCPM	Expected Score Middle of Year > 99 WCPM	Expected Score End of Year > 109 WCPM	State Test Percentile (Avg. is > 15th Percentile)
Samuel Notes: ELL. Speaks English well. Bilingual. Spanish speaker—loves to interact with friends and is typically engaged in class.	56	80	86	35
Luke Notes: A-average in fourth grade. Enjoys science and is able to read chapter books well.	90	116	128	92
Julia Notes: ELL. Difficult to understand. Quiet. Small vocabulary but eager to learn. She is very slow in getting through content and does not ask questions. Interacts infrequently.	30	45	70	10
Ethan Notes: Quiet. Has difficulty with reading. Loves cartoons and math.	60	72	99	5

WCPM = words correct per minute. Hasbrouck & Tindal (2006) recommended guidelines for fifth grade words read correctly in one minute. Hasbrouck, J. & Tindal, G.A. (2006). Oral reading fluency norms: A valuable assessment tool for reading teachers. *The Reading Teacher, 59*(7), 636–644.

FIGURE 7 Fifth Grade CBM Oral Reading Fluency Score in Ms. Cuellar's Class

Struggling Learners

Let's begin by discussing what you may find out about a struggling learner. Struggling learners usually have not been identified as having a disability, but they are performing below average on state assessments and CMBs in reading. Your data will probably show a student who has scored around or below the 15th percentile on the state assessments.

Struggling learners are close to meeting benchmark scores on curriculum-based reading assessments but are not quite there yet. Struggling learners are often reluctant to engage with the curriculum because they feel unsuccessful. Research shows us that struggling learners are at risk of dropping out of school at some point during high school. As a teacher of struggling learners, you need to be (a) creative in engaging them with interesting materials that keep them connected with the curriculum, (b) help them feel successful, and (c) build their reading skills.

Specific Learning Disabilities

What happens if your data search identifies students who have a disability? Students with a reading disability are referred to as having a specific learning disability in the area of reading. These students will likely score well below average on the state assessments and will not meet benchmarks on curriculum-based assessments. If a student is receiving special education supports and services, you will be able to find or ask for a document called an Individualized Educational Plan, or IEP. The IEP tells you what type(s) of disability a student has and also summarizes the student's strengths and weaknesses using both qualitative and quantitative data. It provides a very specific plan for the instruction students need to receive: what type of specialized instruction (e.g., Wilson Learning Services, Orton Gillingham, Project Read—link to http://www.rti4success.org, http://www.nihchcy.org, http://www.cecsped.org), for how long and how often (e.g., 30 minutes, 3 times per week), and by whom. The IEP also describes the types of modifications and accommodations that the student will need to access the curriculum in the regular education classroom and on assessments. You can use the IEP as a roadmap for providing students with effective instruction and accommodations.

English Language Learners

Let's now take a look at English language learners (ELLs) who may be struggling or need a different approach to instruction. You may also have bilingual learners who are learning English. These students are typically called ELLs or limited English proficient. These students can be at different levels of learning English. Most states and districts break down English learning into five or six levels of English language proficiency. This English language proficiency level basically describes how well the English oral language development is improving over time. The most recent measure has been developed by the World-Class Instructional Design and Assessment standards used in many states in the U.S. (http://www.wida.org). Look at your district's website for more information and talk to your ESL teacher for more information.

Find out who will be working with each of your ELLs. Typically, you will be working with the ESL teacher to co-develop lesson plans and integrate the supports they provide. From the ESL teacher, you can ask if the instructional plans you develop need further adaptation for ELLs to access the content. Two really great and fairly easy ways to adapt content for ELLs are (1) label things in your classroom, ideally in multiple languages and English, and (2) design your lessons so that there is an oral presentation, a visual presentation, and a hands-on application so that all students have multiple ways to engage with the curriculum content. The goal is for ELL students to hear content and vocabulary from their teachers and peers, link what they hear to what they see, and then do an activity with the new information so that they can remember it.

We have looked at the types of data you might find and how it relates to your learners. Now let's look at best practices for planning instruction that results in student success.

How Can I Improve My Instructional Practices?

We have learned many approaches to teaching over the last few decades. However, what we have also learned is that we typically teach the way we were taught. How were you taught? Were you in rows with a teacher in front, or did you work in small groups? Let's take some time to reflect, either by yourself or at your common planning time. Think about how you were taught. Make a list of what your experiences have been as a student. Now make a list of the typical ways you teach your students. What are the similarities and differences? Many teachers feel that teaching in front of the classroom is very comfortable for them. They feel in control. Other teachers feel that they would rather handle small groups of students at one time. Some teachers use a combination. So what is the "right" way? How can you get there?

According to researchers in the field of education, instruction should use a variety of flexible grouping practices: whole group, small group, peer pairing, and conferencing. You will want to use these grouping practices for various reasons. And you will want to include opportunities for same-ability grouping and for mixed-ability grouping. All students benefit from a variety of grouping practices for learning, as long as the teacher is clear on the goals and expected outcomes of each approach.

Take a look at Figure 8, which highlights the benefit of these instructional grouping approaches for different types of learners.

Types of Instructional Grouping Approaches	Purpose	Benefit for Struggling Learner	Benefit for ELL	Benefit for Student with Special Education Needs
Whole-class large group instruction. Limitations: not all students at the same level; inability to check for 100% understanding; students not actively engaged but passive learners; attention span is shorter than typical periods in schools; lesson may become oral/auditory only.	Introduce new concept. Activation of prior knowledge. Review academic vocabulary. Teacher introduces content equally to all students. Allows for teacher modeling.	Student is able to hear the concept correctly from the teacher. Student is able to begin linking to prior knowledge.	Student has access to the regular curriculum, builds vocabulary, and activates prior knowledge from others and self. Teacher presents concept orally and visually. Students hear others express academic language orally.	Student has access to the regular curriculum, builds vocabulary, and activates prior knowledge from others and self.
Small-group instruction with same skill-level peers Limitations: teacher has to focus on helping students gain skills or there is a danger of staying at the same level; students may increase skills at different rates.	Review concepts and provide strategy instruction to apply the concepts at students' instructional level. All students are engaged in active learning. Allows for independent learning.	Student works with same skill-level peers, and is able to ask questions from peers and teacher. Student learns from teacher modeling but with direct instruction; student feels success. Students can use a variety of materials at instructional level to slowly progress to grade-level text (i.e., hi-lo books).	Student works with same skill-level peers, is able to ask questions, and learns strategies that are not learned from teacher modeling but only with direct instruction; student feels success. Students can review vocabulary and link it to primary language using strategies, oral language practices. Students can use a variety of materials at instructional level and slowly progress to grade-level text (i.e., hi-lo books).	Student works with same skill-level peers. peers, is able to ask questions, and learns strategies that are not learned from teacher modeling but only with direct instruction; student feels success. Special education teacher can be directing the specialized instruction in this group. Students can use a variety of materials at instructional level and slowly progress to grade-level text (i.e., hi-lo books).

Table continued on p. 33

Types of Instructional Grouping Approaches	Purpose	Benefit for Struggling Learner	Benefit for ELL	Benefit for Student with Special Education Needs
Small-group instruction with mixed-ability levels. Limitations: some students may feel overwhelmed with role or may not be able to communicate effectively; frustration can occur.	Review concepts Opportunity to practice skills Teamwork activities where each member has a role (e.g., recorder, timekeeper, reporter, etc.) All students are engaged in active learning. Allows for independent learning.	Students can have a role that is specific to skill level and feel academic and social success. Student can learn from peers at higher skill levels.	Students can have a role that is specific to skill level and feel academic and social success. Student can learn from peers at higher skill levels (e.g., academic language models, vocabulary, and explanation from various perspectives).	Students can have a role that is specific to skill level and feel academic and social success. Student can learn from peers at higher skill levels.
Student pairing and peer-mediated learning. Limitations: none	Provide specific opportunities for students to be tutor and tutee. Set up in a success format. Excellent for reading fluency and comprehension practice. All students are engaged in active learning. Allows for independent learning in a team.	Student is paired with a peer not too above grade level who can still provide immediate correction. Peer still needs independent practice and provides it as an immediate support to a struggling peer.	Student is paired with a peer not too above grade level who can support English language learning, provide immediate correction on concept, pronunciation, and sentence structure within guided academic discussion. Peer still needs independent practice and provides it as an immediate support to a struggling peer.	Student is paired with a peer not too above grade level who can still provide immediate correction. Peer still needs independent practice and provides it as an immediate support to a struggling peer. Peers work as a successful team using specialized curriculum (i.e., hi-lo books) materials helpful at both students' instructional level.

Table continued on p. 34

Types of Instructional Grouping Approaches	Purpose	Benefit for Struggling Learner	Benefit for ELL	Benefit for Student with Special Education Needs
Teacher conferencing Limitations: none	Relationship building around reading skills. Teacher is able to hear from each student and review potential areas of misunderstanding. Established goals for success.	Struggling students typically don't interact in class. This approach offers struggling learners an opportunity to share their strengths and weaknesses and get clarification from the teacher.	ELLs don't usually interact in whole-group instruction. This offers them an opportunity to share, in English or primary language, their knowledge. Teacher is able to see progress in the content area and English in a lower-stakes situation.	Students who have disabilities don't usually interact in whole-group instruction. This offers them an opportunity to share with their teacher, with ample time to process in a lower-stakes situation. It can include the special education teacher for greater collaboration and progress toward special education goals and standards in regular education.

FIGURE 8 Flexible Grouping Practices

It may seem overwhelming to think about doing all of these approaches, but you can begin introducing one at a time. You typically have one approach you do well, (e.g., whole-group reading instruction), and you can integrate one more (e.g., small-group fluency practice) until you feel successful. You can also visit another colleague's reading class and replicate a small-group guided or independent center or station that you found effective. Try it for about 4 to 6 weeks, then introduce another until you have a variety of active engagement centers or stations. It is also advisable that you provide positive reinforcement for group behavior to foster good teamwork and collaboration in the small groups and/or pairs.

In each classroom diagram in Figure 9, you can see students sitting in small groups of two or four (this can be increased to six for larger class sizes). You can use this layout to teach a whole group or a small group. You also want to ensure collaboration and engagement as a team for teamwork. We would recommend that you provide acknowledgement or positive reinforcement for good group work by offering tangibles that students want. Some good examples of tangibles are five points on the next test, a free homework day, being able to listen to music during independent practice, or popcorn for the table while they work on a Friday.

There are some excellent web-based classroom design tools that allow you to set up your classroom for the most effective learning environment.

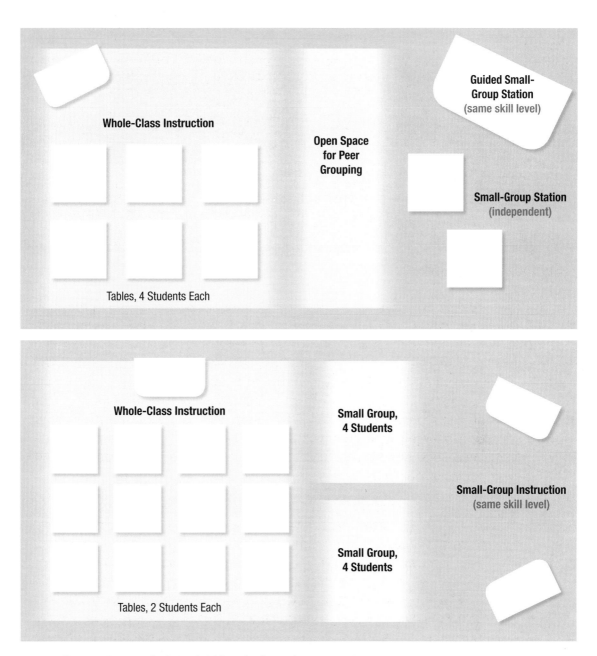

Whole-Class Instruction

Tables, 4 Students Each

Open Space
for Peer
Grouping

Guided Small-
Group Station
(same skill level)

Small-Group Station
(independent)

Whole-Class Instruction

Tables, 2 Students Each

Small Group,
4 Students

Small Group,
4 Students

Small-Group Instruction
(same skill level)

FIGURE 9 Classroom Diagrams for Instructional Grouping Approaches

There are also some grid-based seating charts, which allow you to print and plot your classroom space on paper. When designing your learning environment, what aspect of the design:

- allows for whole-group instruction?

- allows for small-group instruction?

- allows for peer-mediated work?

- allows for conferencing with students?

- provides access to reading materials and resource materials for all students?

- allows for active engagement in the classroom?

- supports good classroom management?

- will welcome diverse learners, including English learners and students with disabilities?

Lesson Plans

Now that you have thought about how to increase learning activities and how you can organize the classroom, let's look at how teaching can be enhanced to address the needs of all students in reading. First, think about whether you complete your lesson plans in reading and English language arts as intended. Do you not get to specific areas, like the review section?

Lesson plans should include a particular set of parts: introduction, activation of prior knowledge, goal setting, direct instruction of concept or standard, guided practice, review, independent practice, and assessment. Although these aspects may be the basic lesson plan format, it is important to also look at district guidance on reading instruction. Typically, districts provide guidance as to the number of minutes of instruction and a breakdown of skills in each content area.

You can also look at research from the National Reading Panel that provides guidance on how to teach reading. The National Reading Panel (2000) suggests that to teach reading, teachers should use techniques that are addressed in these five areas: phonemic awareness, phonics, fluency, vocabulary, and comprehension. Additionally, a study commissioned by the National Literacy Panel on Language-Minority Children and Youth also found that for teaching students who are English learners, teachers should provide instruction that addresses oral language development in addition to the five areas. Focusing on these six areas of reading, teachers can ensure that high-quality reading instruction is provided to all students in any diverse classroom (August and Shanahan, 2006).

As your students develop reading skills, consider this shift, which usually occurs between third and fourth grade. Educators often say that kindergarten to third grade focuses on learning how to read, while third grade and up is reading to learn (content). This shift applies in cases where you have ELLs, struggling readers, and students with special education needs.

Take Ms. Cuellar's student Ethan, who scored at the 5th percentile in the state annual test (see Figure 7) and is struggling with reading grade-level content. Ms. Cuellar's planning should consider the instruction and practice Ethan needs in learning how to read in addition to the typical reading to learn expected in upper elementary school in preparation for middle school. Based on his oral reading fluency scores and her observations of Ethan's reading, she will need to adjust the reading practice to include phonemic awareness activities and decoding strategies. She must also provide Ethan with ample opportunities to practice fluency and comprehension, starting with materials right below his grade level and moving toward fifth grade level reading materials as his words read correctly score increases, showing he is able to read grade-level materials efficiently and effectively.

Middle School

Of course, middle school teachers do not think of teaching phonics, decoding, or phonemic awareness. This is because most middle school students have already learned to read and are now building content knowledge. However, we want to provide you with information on all areas of reading instruction because students are not coming well-prepared to middle school. And, in fact, you should be aware of the prerequisite skills students need to have to do grade-level work. You also need to see how these areas of reading look like in middle school. They don't go away but evolve into more developed skills. You can always go back to basics when you have students who are having difficulty reading, gaining vocabulary, decoding, and have poor comprehension. All areas should be taught during a lesson. A mix provides a balanced approach. Lower readers need more practice with learning decoding and phonemic awareness strategies to build fluency. More developed readers need practice on fluent and accurate reading and vocabulary instruction that can support comprehension.

Hi-Lo Books Support Instruction

As we discussed, your lesson plans should address the students in front of you, not your target grade. Your curriculum materials should support your differentiated plans and provide a variety of options for students at different skill levels in order to learn to read and read to learn. Materials can include hi-lo books, emergent readers, leveled readers, and others. What is critical is that you choose age-appropriate materials. For example, Ms. Cuellar does not want her fifth graders reading first grade books because it will make the students feel uncomfortable and babyish. Further, first grade content will not be interesting to fifth graders. So, how does she meet the needs of her struggling learners, ELLs, and students with special education needs? What materials can help them learn, make them feel comfortable, and remain interested so that they want to keep reading and learning?

Hi-lo books offer students the opportunity to read age-appropriate content written at lower reading levels, meaning that students with lower reading skills can read the same content with less text complexity. Hi-lo books for struggling learners, ELLs, and students with disabilities have also been developed with increasing reading levels. For example, if Ms. Cuellar is teaching a lesson on a particular chapter book in the fifth grade, she also has access to the same or similar content in second, third, and fourth grade reading levels so that she can differentiate her instruction in her small groups and in independent practice. The goal should always be on monitoring the progress of reading skills so that you can use hi-lo books to increase text complexity based on reading level.

Fidelity of Implementation

What should a 90-minute reading and English language arts lesson look like so that it addresses the recommended six areas of reading using differentiated curriculum materials? Figure 10 offers an example of what Ms. Cuellar has been developing.

This is a great start for Ms. Cuellar to address the six areas of reading instruction using a variety of teaching approaches with flexible same- and mixed-level groups. However, this plan is only effective if she actually follows through with it. If you don't have a 90-minute period but instead you have a block schedule, then you can break down the minutes, which is what is really recommended, then spread it over your 120-hour block period or

Area of Reading and CCSS	Instructional Approach	Curriculum Materials	Minutes
Phonemic awareness is the ability to hear, identify, and manipulate individual sounds.	Whole group. Oral segmentation, rhyming, blending, deleting, transposing, or sounds (example, T-a-p, t-r-a p, t-a r-p).	Software-based technology Game: rhyming words in pairs or small groups Game: creating words by adding, deleting, transposing, or inserting new sounds	15 min
Phonics is understanding the relationship between letters and sounds, while decoding is the ability to correctly pronounce written words.	Whole and small group, same skill level. Scope and sequence of any purchased curriculum. Using peer-mediated and corrective feedback when decoding unrecognizable words. Add words to a dictionary box or ring.	Hi-lo books Basal readers E-books with read-aloud option	15 min
Fluency refers to how a student reads text with accuracy, intonation, and stress, and pauses as informed by the mechanics of sentences.	Whole-group choral reading, small-group independent practice, repeated reading, peer reading at mixed reading levels. Practice fiction and nonfiction reading selections at independent reading level and at instructional level with supports.	Hi-lo books Emergent readers Leveled libraries Literature: chapter books Basal reader E-books	20 min
Comprehension is the ability to read and understand text through decoding, activating prior knowledge, and thinking critically about what has been read.	Small-group guided practice at same skill level, independent reading, paired reading at mixed-skill level. Practice fiction and nonfiction reading selections at independent reading level and at instructional level with supports, including strategy instruction.	Hi-lo books Emergent readers Leveled libraries Literature: chapter books Basal reader E-books	20 min
Vocabulary refers to knowledge of words and word meanings.	Whole-group choral reading, small group at same skill level, independent practice, paired reading at mixed-skill level. Direct instruction of vocabulary of basal reader or literature book or any other materials used. Vocabulary has academic language and content language.	Hi-lo books Emergent readers Leveled libraries Literature: chapter books Basal reader E-books with hypertext; student records words into personal dictionary	10 min

Table continued on p. 40

Area of Reading and CCSS	Instructional Approach	Curriculum Materials	Minutes
Oral language development	Whole and small group at same and mixed-skill levels. Direct instruction of oral language interaction, visualizing and connecting to the context of the lesson.	Hi-lo books Emergent readers Leveled libraries Literature: chapter books Basal reader E-books with read-aloud option or scan pen	10 min

FIGURE 10 Ms. Cuellar's Weekly 90-Minute Reading Block

your 45-minute block period. The idea is that the planning addresses all areas of reading so that students can have all skills needed to access the grade-level curriculum. Now remember, doing the plan as she intended is key. This is called "fidelity of implementation."

Fidelity of Implementation

Fidelity of implementation occurs when teachers use the instructional strategies and deliver the content of the curriculum in the same way that they were designed to be used and delivered.

Take a different example from your life. Let's imagine you wanted to run in a four-mile race 1 month from now. You design a plan. Week 1 you run one mile every day. Week 2 it's two miles every day. Week 3 it's three miles every day. And Week 4 it's four miles every day until race day.

The plan sounds great. And you run for 4 days. Then you take a few days off. Some days you don't feel like waking up early. Some days you work late. These types of interruptions happen at least a few times per week. When race day arrives, you are not ready because you have not implemented your plan with fidelity. More importantly, you did not develop a realistic and doable plan.

This is the same type of thinking that must apply to instructional delivery. Teachers need to implement curriculum and instruction with fidelity so that students make progress and achieve success.

Fidelity of implementation plays a crucial role in packaged curriculum, like basal readers, specialized curriculum, or hi-lo books. All packaged curriculum has been evaluated, and teachers should follow the recommended application so that students get the practice they need. For example, in using hi-lo books, you should always monitor progress in reading fluency and comprehension at least 3 times per year so that the students are reading challenging materials that approach grade-level content in both fiction and nonfiction.

If you are not using a packaged curriculum and the school you work at has you develop the content, make sure that you follow a balanced approach to reading instruction. You and your colleagues in the same grade should share best practices and address each area similarly. Collaborating in this manner will diminish the potential of having students not get enough practice in any given area and will improve their chances of moving up to the next grade level with the skills needed to be successful readers.

Using a self-assessment chart is a great way to track that you have addressed all six areas of reading instruction every day. A "Reading Instruction Teacher Self-Assessment" sample chart can be found in the Appendix. Work with other teachers during a common planning time to discuss what challenges came up and how they were solved. This exchange of ideas builds fidelity of implementation of your common expectations for your students, their parents, and the school. Linking back to RTI, this ensures that Tier 1 (core) instruction is strong and reaching most of your students (75%–85%).

How Do I Know Whether Students Are Learning from My Instruction?

As you move from who your students are, based on data; what instructional delivery should involve, what reading instruction should address; and how to maintain fidelity of implementation, you must think about how to monitor what your students are learning. *Progress monitoring* and *universal screening* refers to a practice of using quick checks, or indicators, that tell you whether students are making progress on grade-level content.

Think back to the beginning of the chapter when we described district assessments. CBMs are quick skill checks that take as little as 3–5 minutes per student. You should conduct curriculum-based assessments for all students at least 3 times per year to get a sense of their skills in addition to your typical end-of-chapter tests and activities. Remember CBMs tells you at any point whether the students have the reading skills to access the great curriculum and content you are teaching.

For struggling learners, ELLs, and students with disabilities, you should administer curriculum-based assessments much more frequently—monthly or even weekly—to see whether they are responding to the instructional approach. Your district may have purchased tools like DIBELS or AIMSweb, which are popular curriculum-based assessments that provide teachers with benchmarks of how students should be reading at the beginning, middle, and end of the school year.

Educators can also create their own curriculum-based assessments by asking students to read for 1 minute from curriculum that is being used in the classroom. Count the number of words read correctly, which will give you an indication of the student's rate of reading. You divide words read correctly by the total number of words to get a percentage that indicates how accurately the student is reading. Over time, you want the student's rate and accuracy to increase. You can administer curriculum-based assessments as frequently as needed to determine how much progress or lack of progress a student is making. If a student's rate and accuracy are not improving over time (4–6 weeks of static or decreasing scores), this is an indication that you need to adjust instruction.

A Quick Curriculum-Based Assessment Using Hi-Lo Books

You can use hi-lo books to create curriculum-based assessments. If you have a student reading below grade level, pre-select a passage where you have already counted the total number of words. Have the student read aloud for 1 minute to determine rate and accuracy. Note the number of words read incorrectly.

The text sample page is from Saddleback Publishing's *I'm Just Me,* by M. G. Higgins, a hi-lo book for the middle grades and YA written at Lexile level 390L. Notice the word count tally on the far right of the sample page. The formula to determine reading accuracy is Total Word Count *minus* Words Read Incorrectly. Then the Difference *divided* by Total Word Count.

Example, 144 (Total Word Count) minus 25 (Words Read Incorrectly) = 119 (Difference). 119 (Difference) divided by 144 (Total Word Count) = 82.6. The student reads with approximately 83% accuracy.

	Chapter 11	
"She's calling me bad names!" Kyle	6	
whines.	7	
The driver glares at us. "Cool it. Or I'll	16	
write you both up."	20	
The bus door closes. By now, there	27	
are no empty seats. Mia and I have to sit	37	
with other people. My heart is beating like	45	
a rabbit's. I can barely catch my breath. I	54	
can't believe I said that to Kyle. What was	63	
I thinking?	65	
I feel a hand on my shoulder. I tense	74	
up. But then I hear Mia whisper, "That	82	
was awesome."	84	
I nod. But if it was so awesome, why	93	
am I trembling? At least I'm not sitting	101	
next to Kyle, taking his verbal abuse.	108	
He keeps turning and staring. Puckering	114	
his lips. I look out the window and force	123	
myself to breathe.	126	
My heart is still skipping when we	133	
walk into school. I can't seem to take	141	
deep-enough breaths.	144	
81		

Typically students gain one word per week in fluency. There are 30 weeks in the school year, so you use that as a way to guide how much progress a student should be making. If Ms. Cuellar has a student who is currently reading 30 words per minute, like Julia, and she is using a hi-lo book to support reading instruction, the teacher can expect her to grow approximately one word per week. By the end of 30 weeks of school, she can potentially be reading 60 words correctly per minute. This represents a typical growth pattern, even though it would not be at grade level. If your instruction is working well and your student is progressing faster than expected, you should consider more challenging material at an increased reading level.

Summary

In this chapter, we described how to use different types of data to learn about your students. We suggested that qualitative and quantitative data can help you develop an instructional approach that is effective and engaging. We asked you to start to think about profiles of struggling learners, ELLs, and students with special education needs. We acknowledged how challenging it can be to create a balanced approach to reading instruction that meets the needs of so many different students. We provided you with examples of instructional delivery models and a 90-minute reading block that is balanced and engaging. We described how to select materials that complement your instructional approaches and make students feel comfortable, interested, and successful. Finally, we offered ways for you to make sure your students are learning.

In the next chapter, we will learn more about each of Ms. Cuellar's students. We will take a detailed look at profiles of her struggling learners, ELLs, and students with disabilities, and we will discuss how to support them on a daily basis using specific instructional strategies. We will describe what happens when these learners don't respond to instruction and will describe exactly what to do when this happens.

CHAPTER 3

Instructional Interventions That Work

In Chapter 2, we learned about how Ms. Cuellar uses data to understand her students. We provided you with examples of instructional delivery models and a 90-minute reading block that is balanced and academically engaging. We described how to select materials that complement your instructional approaches and make students feel comfortable, interested, engaged, and successful.

In this chapter, we take a closer look at Ms. Cuellar's struggling students. We will learn how to provide tiered instruction that meets the needs of different types of learners. As you read the student profiles, remember there are six key components of reading instruction in which students may have one or more difficulties. The six areas are phonemic awareness, phonics, fluency, comprehension, vocabulary, and oral language development. We showcase a "how to intervene" on the most common areas of reading difficulty. Figure 11 illustrates a quick guide to each area of reading difficulty covered in this chapter, and the strategy we will present.

Area of Reading Difficulty	Name of Strategy	Recommended Delivery	Facilitator	Page
Fluency	Partner Reading, Tier 1 or 2	Pairs	Targeted Peer Group	47
Comprehension	Shrink It!, Tier 1 or 2	Pairs	Targeted Peer Group	51
Fluency and Vocabulary	Boom!, Tier 1 or 2	Small Group, 2–4 Students	Teacher or Volunteer	54
Comprehension	Collaborative Strategic Reading, Tier 1 or 2	Small Group, 4–5 Students	Targeted Peer Group	57
Fluency and Vocabulary	Incremental Rehearsal, Tier 2 or 3	1:1	Teacher or Volunteer	61
Decoding and Comprehension	Supported Cloze Procedure, Tier 3	1:1	Teacher or Volunteer	63

FIGURE 11 Strategy Quick Guide

⦾A Look Inside the Classroom

Now let's remind ourselves about some of the students in Ms. Cuellar's classroom this year using Figure 12.

Student	Expected Score Beginning of Year > 85 WCPM	Expected Score Middle of Year > 99 WCPM	Expected Score End of Year > 109 WCPM	State Test Percentile (Avg. is > 15th Percentile)
Samuel Notes: ELL. Speaks English well. Bilingual. Spanish speaker—loves to interact with friends and is typically engaged in class.	56	80	86	35
Luke Notes: A-average in fourth grade. Enjoys science and is able to read chapter books well.	90	116	128	92
Julia Notes: ELL. Difficult to understand. Quiet. Small vocabulary but eager to learn. She is very slow in getting through content and does not ask questions. Interacts infrequently.	30	45	70	10
Ethan Notes: Quiet. Has difficulty with reading. Loves cartoons and math.	60	72	99	5

WCPM = words correct per minute. Hasbrouck & Tindal (2006) recommended guidelines for fifth grade words read correctly in one minute. Hasbrouck, J. & Tindal, G.A. (2006). Oral reading fluency norms: A valuable assessment tool for reading teachers. *The Reading Teacher, 59*(7), 636–644.

FIGURE 12 Fifth Grade CBM Oral Reading Fluency Score in Ms. Cuellar's Class

Ms. Cuellar has 24 fifth grade students with many different instructional needs. Some of her students are reading at a third grade level, and others are reading closer to an eighth grade level. Let's consider some of the supplemental Tier 2 and Tier 3 instructional interventions that she can put into place for her struggling students. Some of these practices can also be built into your high-quality Tier 1 (core) reading block. In this chapter, you will learn exactly how to implement the following interventions: Partner Reading targets reading fluency (Tier 1 or 2); Shrink It! targets reading comprehension (Tier 1 or 2); Boom! A Sight Word Intervention targets reading fluency and vocabulary (Tier 1 or 2); Collaborative Strategic Reading includes four strategies that target reading comprehension (Tier 1 or 2); Incremental Rehearsal targets reading fluency and vocabulary (Tier 2 or 3); Supported Cloze Procedure targets reading accuracy (decoding) and comprehension (Tier 3).

Partner Reading
Tier 1 or Tier 2 Intervention Strategy
◉ TARGETS READING FLUENCY

Samuel is a bilingual Spanish speaker who is reading below grade level. He is what we would call a "struggling reader." His benchmark scores indicate he struggles with reading fluency, which likely also impacts his reading comprehension. Ms. Cuellar knows Samuel loves working with friends and wants to succeed in school. For a student like Samuel, you may want to start with a peer-mediated activity such as Partner Reading, which is designed to improve fluency.

This intervention draws from the principles of Peer-Assisted Learning Strategies (Fuchs, Fuchs, Mathes, & Simmons, 1997) and does not require special curriculum materials. Partner Reading pairs students in a systematic way. This strategy uses classroom materials at various levels to differentiate each pairs' needs. Lower readers can use hi-lo books at their particular reading level.

What Is Tiered Instruction?

Remember, Tier 1 refers to the high-quality, differentiated core reading instruction that *all* students receive. Tier 2 interventions are delivered in a teacher–student ratio of 1:6 or fewer and are in addition to Tier 1 (core) instruction. Tier 2 interventions should be provided for 20 minutes, 3 times per week. Tier 3 interventions are more intensive and in addition to Tier 1 and ideally Tier 2. Tier 3 interventions are delivered in a teacher–student ratio of 1:3 or fewer. Tier 3 interventions should be provided daily for 30 minutes. Tier 2 and Tier 3 interventions should never replace high-quality Tier 1 (core) instruction but should be provided *in addition* to it.

Strategy Description

Partner Reading is a peer-assisted strategy for use in classrooms to improve student proficiency in reading fluency and accuracy. Partner Reading can be used with students with diverse academic needs, including gifted learners, ELLs, struggling learners, and students with and without disabilities.

FIGURE 13 Partner Reading Is a Peer-Mediated Strategy

The intervention uses peer-mediated instruction, a process whereby students work in pairs to provide assistance with fluent reading. Students are taught to correct their partner's reading errors and provide consistent reinforcement and feedback.

Recommended Delivery

Partner Reading occurs as a whole-class Tier 1 (core) instructional approach or as a Tier 2 intervention. As a Tier 2 intervention, it should be implemented 3 times per week for at least 20 minutes per session. The strategy is peer-mediated and occurs as an interaction between two peers. Pairs can sit at desks, on the floor as appropriate, or in the hallway or other areas of the building, if it makes sense. To set the stage for success you must:

- establish a routine for students to adopt so that they know the step-by-step requirements for engaging in paired reading.

- think about seating and where the materials will be located for Partner Reading time.

- identify appropriate reading selections. The reading selection should reflect the reading level of the lower-level reader. Consider using hi-lo books because they are engaging and accessible.

Facilitator

Partner Reading is a peer-mediated strategy, so the students act as facilitators of learning. At the outset, the teacher will model the strategy for students so that they learn how to provide feedback in a structured and corrective way.

Teacher Preparation

Pair high-level readers with low-level readers. Use the following steps:

1. Write a list of students in order from highest to lowest according to reading ability.

2. Divide the list in half.

3. Place the first student on the first list with the first student on the second list.

4. Continue until all students have been partnered as in Figure 14.

High-Performing Readers (HP)	Low-Performing Readers (LP)	Pairs
1st HP	1st LP	A
2nd HP	2nd LP	B
3rd HP	3rd LP	C
4th HP	4th LP	D
5th HP	5th LP	E
6th HP	6th LP	F
7th HP	7th LP	G
8th HP	8th LP	H

FIGURE 14 Partner Reading Pairs

The reader from the first list is known as Partner 1. The reader from the second list is known as Partner 2. Partner 1 always begins the reading, while the Partner 2 listens and follows along. Be sensitive to pairings of students with special needs, including learning or emotional needs. Adjust pairings as necessary.

Directions for Implementing

Provide students with specific steps for what to do:

1. Partner 1, the higher-level reader, reads the first paragraph. Partner 2 follows along.

2. Partner 2, the lower-level reader, reads the same paragraph.

3. After both partners have read one paragraph, Partner 2 will retell what happened in that paragraph in the order that things happened.

4. Partner 1 should say, "Very good!" when Partner 2 retells what happened in that paragraph in the proper order.

5. The pairs will repeat steps 1–4 until the passage is complete.

6. Partners should refer to the Correction Card as needed when a mistake is made.

Corrections

Both students should use the Correction Card in the Appendix, as demonstrated below, to provide assistance when a partner is stuck on a word.

1. If a student reads a word incorrectly, skips a word, or does not say a word within 4 seconds, his or her partner says, "Check it!"

2. Then his or her partner will point to the word and say, "What is this word?"

3. If the student reads the word correctly, the partner says, "Yes, that word is _____. What word?" The student repeats the word. Then the partner says, "Please reread the sentence."

4. Alternatively, if the student does not know the word, the partner says, "That word is _____. What word?" The student says the word. Then the partner says, "Please reread the sentence."

5. The student is always asked to repeat the word and reread the sentence.

Adaptations

Partner 1 and Partner 2 can also make flashcards of all words that Partner 2 does not know. If after reading there are a few extra minutes available, Partner 1 can take five of the cards and review them with Partner 2.

Shrink It!

Tier 1 or Tier 2 Intervention Strategy
⊙ **TARGETS READING COMPREHENSION**

Ms. Cuellar also wants to help Samuel improve his reading comprehension. Once Samuel becomes familiar with the Partner Reading strategy, she decides to add Shrink It! This intervention is designed to improve comprehension and draws from the principles of Peer-Assisted Learning Strategies (Fuchs et al., 1997) and does not require special curriculum materials. In Shrink It! students must state the main idea in 10 words or less, which encourages them to display and monitor comprehension while taking turns reading one paragraph at a time.

Strategy Description

Shrink It! is a peer-assisted strategy for use in classrooms to improve student proficiency in reading comprehension. The strategy allows each student to take turns reading, pausing, and summarizing the main points of each paragraph or page selection, depending on the student's level. Students provide each other with feedback as a way to monitor comprehension.

Recommended Delivery

Shrink It! occurs as a whole-class Tier 1 (core) instructional approach or as a Tier 2 intervention. As a Tier 2 intervention, it should be implemented 3 times per week for at least 20 minutes per session. The strategy is peer-mediated and occurs as an interaction between two peers. Pairs can sit at desks, on the floor as appropriate, or in the hallway or other areas of the building, if it makes sense. To set the stage for success you must:

- establish a routine for students to adopt so that they know the step-by-step requirements for engaging in Shrink It!

- think about seating and where materials will be located for Shrink It! time.

- identify appropriate reading selections. The reading selection should reflect the reading level of the lower-level reader. Consider using hi-lo books because they are engaging and accessible.

Facilitator

Shrink It! is a peer-mediated strategy, so the students act as facilitators of learning. At the outset, the teacher will model the strategy for students so that they learn how to provide feedback in a structured and corrective way.

Teacher Preparation

As in Partner Reading, pair high-level readers with low-level readers. Use the following steps:

1. Write a list of students in order from highest to lowest according to reading ability.

2. Divide the list in half.

3. Place the first student on the first list with the first student on the second list.

4. Continue until all students have been partnered as in Figure 15.

High-Performing Readers (HP)	Low-Performing Readers (LP)	Pairs
1st HP	1st LP	A
2nd HP	2nd LP	B
3rd HP	3rd LP	C
4th HP	4th LP	D
5th HP	5th LP	E
6th HP	6th LP	F
7th HP	7th LP	G
8th HP	8th LP	H

FIGURE 15 Shrink It! Pairs

The reader from the first list is known as Partner 1. The reader from the second list is known as Partner 2. Partner 1 always begins the reading, while Partner 2 listens and follows along. Be sensitive to pairings of students with special needs, including learning or emotional needs. Adjust pairings as necessary.

Directions for Implementing

Choose the assigned reading and introduce the text to the students. Model the following steps to ensure that students understand:

1. Each student reads a paragraph aloud without rereading the same text.

2. After each paragraph, Partner 2 should stop to summarize the main points of the reading. Partner 1 should then ask Partner 2 to summarize the following information:
   a. The main who or what of the paragraph.

      i. Partner 1 should suggest that the main who or what will always be a person, place, thing, or animal.

      ii. If Partner 2 says too many whos or whats, Partner 1 should say, "Remember to choose the *most* important who or what."

   b. The most important thing about who or what.

      i. Partner 1 can provide a hint if needed.

      ii. If Partner 2 ever gives an incorrect answer, Partner 1 should ask him or her to skim the paragraph again and answer the question.

   c. The main idea in 10 words or less.

      i. Partner 1 asks Partner 2 to state the main idea in 10 words or less.

      ii. If Partner 2 uses more than 10 words, Partner 1 says, "Shrink it!"

3. Partners should refer to the Correction Card as needed when a mistake is made.

Corrections

Partner 1 should use the Correction Card in the Appendix to provide assistance if Partner 2 gives an incorrect answer.

1. If Partner 2 gives an incorrect answer, Partner 1 will say, "Try again!"

2. If Partner 2 gives another incorrect answer, Partner 1 will say, "Here's a hint"

3. If Partner 2 still cannot answer correctly, Partner 1 will say, "The answer is _____."

4. Alternatively, if Partner 2 uses more than 10 words for the main idea, Partner 1 says, "Shrink it!"

Adaptations

Students can summarize paragraphs or longer chunks of text as appropriate. For example, high school students may be ready to use this strategy at the end of a page of text as opposed to a paragraph.

Boom! A Sight Word Intervention
Tier 1 or Tier 2 Intervention Strategy
⊙ TARGETS READING FLUENCY AND VOCABULARY

Julia's scores on benchmark and state assessments tell Ms. Cuellar that she is a struggling reader. In addition, she is an ELL, has a small vocabulary, and struggles with sight words. Ms. Cuellar wants to focus on helping students like Julia build their sight word recognition and vocabulary.

Boom! is an engaging and playful Tier 2 intervention that can be adapted to address sight words (e.g., the most commonly occurring words that appear at the student's instructional or grade level), vocabulary, and spelling. Sight words are words that appear in at least 75% of the content that students read in the curriculum. For struggling readers, not knowing these words slows them down when reading because they are trying to decode each word. It is important to have students practice sight words and to have teachers monitor how many sight words students are adding to their sight word vocabulary. Struggling readers often do not have these words in their repertoire.

Some examples of sight words can be found in your existing curriculum. Sometimes they are presented ahead of time in books students read. You can also obtain them on educational websites. Fry and Dolch are two popular sight word lists. Typically, students in kindergarten to second grade learn about 200 sight words per year. Then each year after, there are graded lists that are also recommended.

Strategy Description

The Boom! intervention strategy is a fun and fast-paced game in which the object is for the student to say as many sight words as he or she can.

Recommended Delivery

Boom! occurs as a whole-class Tier 1 (core) instructional approach or as a Tier 2 intervention. As a Tier 2 intervention, it should be implemented 3 times per week for at least 20 minutes per session. The strategy occurs among a small group of peers, with a teacher or volunteer facilitating the game and providing feedback as needed. Groups can sit at small circular tables or at desks pushed together to make a larger area.

Think about developing a routine for delivering the Boom! strategy, which includes:

- identifying sight words lists. Consider differentiating by Tier 1 (core), Tier 2, and Tier 3 sight words. Consult your hi-lo books for examples of sight words, or review Dolch or Fry lists. Determine a way of assessing student mastery of sight words, i.e., when to incorporate new words.

- writing sight words on wooden craft sticks.

- storing the sticks in a container (e.g., coffee can, jar, basket).

- establishing a routine for students to adopt so that they know the step-by-step requirements for engaging in Boom!

- thinking about seating and where materials will be located for Boom!

Facilitator

Boom! is a small group game facilitated by a teacher or volunteer. The teacher or volunteer will show the students how to play the game and will provide corrective feedback as needed.

Teacher Preparation

1. Write high-frequency sight words on wooden craft sticks (one word per stick).

2. Develop lists of Tier 1 (core), Tier 2, and Tier 3 sight words.

3. On several sticks, write the word, "Boom!"

4. Place sticks in a container or basket.

Directions for Implementing

The teacher should provide these directions for students:

1. Students sit in a circle.

2. Students take turns picking a stick and reading the word fluently.

3. If the student reads the word correctly, the stick is kept.

4. If student reads the word incorrectly, the stick goes back into the container.

FIGURE 16 Sight Words on Wooden Craft Sticks

5. When a student chooses a Boom! stick, he or she must say, "Boom!" and put all of his or her word sticks back into the container.

6. The player with the most sticks wins.

Corrections

None

Adaptations

Teachers can adapt this game for both spelling and vocabulary words. The game can also be made into a writing connection by asking the students to write a sentence using the word. In those variations, students would have to spell or define the word they chose. Teachers can also periodically replace the Boom! sticks with sticks that match the classroom tangibles, such as a free homework pass, 2 points on an exam, or extra points to reinforce social interaction skills or task completion, etc.

Teachers may create a container with harder words for stronger readers and a container with word–picture cards to provide full support for students with special needs. Word–picture cards are also key for ELLs who need visual connections to new words so that they use their first language and connect it to an object with the new word in English.

Collaborative Strategic Reading
Tier 1 or Tier 2 Intervention Strategy
⊙ **TARGETS READING COMPREHENSION**

In Ms. Cuellar's class, there are 24 students whose reading comprehension levels vary quite a bit. Consider the challenge of teaching a reading group with a variety of learners like Luke, Julia, Ethan, and Samuel. You may have this type of diversity in your own classroom and wonder how to plan instruction for such a wide range of learning profiles.

Ms. Cuellar wants to incorporate an instructional strategy that will help all of her students improve their comprehension and stay engaged and interested in reading. She decides to implement Collaborative Strategic Reading (Klingner & Vaughn, 1998), which is a set of four strategies that readers can use to decode and comprehend as they read content area text.

Strategy Description

Collaborative Strategic Reading (CSR) (Klingner & Vaughn, 1998) is a set of four strategies that readers can use to cooperatively decode and comprehend as they read content area text. CSR can be used by content area teachers in inclusion settings as well as by reading teachers. To implement CSR, students of mixed reading and achievement levels work in small cooperative groups of 4–5 students. They support each other in applying a sequence of four reading strategies as they read orally or silently from a shared selection of text.

Recommended Delivery

CSR occurs as a whole-class Tier 1 (core) instructional approach or as a Tier 2 intervention. As a Tier 2 intervention, it should be implemented 3 times per week for at least 20 minutes per session. The strategy occurs among 4–5 peers who have been strategically grouped based on skills.

The teacher introduces the reading selection using a preview strategy, and then the group works together to develop their understanding of the selection. Groups can sit at small circular tables or at desks pushed together to make a larger area. You will then want to think about developing a routine for delivering CSR, which includes:

- ensuring that students know the step-by-step requirements for engaging in CSR.
- creating a CSR table in your classroom where role cue cards are laminated and taped onto specific seats. This way, students know where to sit and can reference the cue cards as needed.

Facilitator

CSR is a small group intervention where peers assist each other in developing improved reading comprehension. A teacher introduces and previews the reading selection, and then the group works together to build their understanding.

Teacher Preparation

Teachers must identify the reading passages that students will use while working in CSR groups. CSR can be used across all content areas. In English language arts, hi-lo books are an excellent choice because they are available at many different reading levels and have content that engages all readers. Teachers may also use content area science or social studies texts.

Teachers must then develop the groups of 4–5 students. To learn to work in a cooperative group, students are taught the following roles, which correspond to the strategies:

- Leader, who says what to read next and what strategy to apply next.
- Clunk Expert, who uses cards to remind the group of the steps.
- Gist Expert, who guides the group to articulate the gist and then evaluates it.
- Announcer, who calls upon group members to read or share ideas.
- Encourager, who gives praise.

Each role has a cue card in the Appendix, which explains exactly how to perform the responsibilities of the role. For example, the cue card for Clunk Expert prompts "What is your clunk? Does anyone know the meaning of the clunk?" With this in mind, you can select which students would be appropriate for each role.

In Ms. Cuellar's case, she decides to assign Luke as the Leader *and* Clunk Expert. Samuel will be the Gist Expert. Ethan will be the Announcer.

Julia will be the Encourager. Each student gains social skills through this collaborative interaction. Although Luke is already a strong reader, by guiding his group through fixing up the "Clunks," he is reinforcing and internalizing his strong reading strategies. Julia, Ethan, and Samuel are getting practice in applying strategies that will improve their comprehension. When making your decisions about groupings for CSR, you may want to rank your students from the strongest to the weakest reader.

CSR Group	Clunk Expert	Leader	Gist Expert	Announcer	Encourager
A	1 (Strongest Reader)	5	9	13	17
B	2	6	10	14	18
C	3	7	11	15	19
D	4	8	12	16	20 (Weakest Reader)

FIGURE 17 CSR Grouping

In Figure 17, there are four CSR groups (A–D). In each group, the strongest reader is taking the role of Clunk Expert. The next highest reader takes the role of Leader. The middle reader, who may be a struggling reader, takes the role of Gist Expert, and the very struggling readers are assigned as Announcer and Encourager.

CSR in four steps:

1. Preview. Students preview the entire passage before reading each section to:
   a. build and activate background knowledge.
   b. learn as much about the passage as they can in a brief period of time.
   c. help make predictions about what they will learn.
   d. motivate interest in the topic and to engage them in active reading from the onset.

2. Click and Clunk. Students identify words or word parts during reading that make sense or "click," and that were hard to understand (called "clunks"). Students click and clunk to:
   a. monitor their reading comprehension.
   b. identify when they have breakdowns in understanding.

c. use "fix-up" strategies to figure out clunks.

   i. Three fix-up strategies are:

      1. Use context clues. Reread the sentence without the word and think about what would make sense. Read around the sentence with the clunk and look for clues.

      2. Conduct a word analysis. Look for a prefix, root, or suffix in the word. Break the word apart and look for smaller words you know.

      3. Clarify the concept. Identify the part of the passage that is not clear. Discuss the passage to clarify with the CSR group.

3. Get the Gist. Students restate the most important point as a way of making sure they have understood what they have read. Students identify the following information:

   a. most important idea in a section of text (usually a paragraph).

   b. most important person, place, or thing.

   c. most important idea about the person, place, or thing.

4. Wrap Up. After reading, students construct their own questions to check for understanding of the passage, answer the questions, and summarize what has been learned.

Directions for Implementing

The teacher should provide these directions:

1. The teacher introduces the topic, teaches key vocabulary, and provides instructions.

2. Cooperative group activity using the Preview, Click and Clunk, Get the Gist, and Wrap Up strategies. Each group member plays an assigned role (e.g., Leader, Clunk Expert) and fills out a CSR Learning Log during the activity. All CSR logs, cue cards, and clunk cards are located in the Appendix.

3. Whole-class summary. The teacher discusses the day's reading passage, reviews clunks, answers questions, and shares some review ideas.

Corrections

None

Adaptations

For groups in which all learners are struggling, consider assigning a teacher or paraprofessional to the role of Leader and Clunk Expert.

Incremental Rehearsal
Tier 2 or Tier 3 Intervention Strategy
⊚ TARGETS READING FLUENCY AND VOCABULARY

Julia and Ethan both struggle with vocabulary. They tend to remember vocabulary words for a short time but cannot retain them and generalize the academic vocabulary that is necessary for comprehension. To continue to build their knowledge of academic vocabulary, Ms. Cuellar decides to implement the Incremental Rehearsal intervention (Petersen-Brown & Burns, 2011), which is a Tier 2 or Tier 3 intervention intended to develop fluency with previously learned skills and build familiarity with unknown concepts.

Strategy Description

The Incremental Rehearsal technique is a drill ratio procedure designed to intersperse a ratio of unknown content (10%) to known content (90%), such as words and word meanings. A student is presented with flashcards containing unknown items added into a group of known items. Specifically, Incremental Rehearsal consists of identifying nine words that students have mastered. These words are classified as "known" words. The instructor also identifies 10 words that the student cannot read, and these are classified as "unknown" words. Presenting known information along with unknown allows for high rates of success and can increase retention of the newly learned items.

Recommended Delivery

Incremental Rehearsal is an individualized Tier 2 or Tier 3 intervention where the interaction occurs in a student–teacher ratio of 1:1. As a Tier 2 intervention, it should be implemented 3 times per week for at least 20 minutes per session. As a Tier 3 intervention, it should be implemented daily for 20–30 minutes. The strategy occurs between one student and a teacher or volunteer. The student and teacher can sit together at a desk or table. The intervention could occur in the general classroom or in another area of the school, if it makes more sense.

You will then want to think about developing a routine for delivering the Incremental Rehearsal strategy. This may include the following:

- Ensure that students know the step-by-step requirements for engaging in Incremental Rehearsal.

- Think about seating and where materials will be located.

- Determine lists of words or concepts to include.

Facilitator

Incremental Rehearsal is teacher-facilitated. A teacher provides feedback as the student progresses through the stack of words or concepts.

Teacher Preparation

Write nine known words on flashcards and 10 unknown words on flashcards. Consider using Tier 2 or Tier 3 words depending on the student's instructional level.

Directions for Implementing

1. Take nine cards from the "known" stack and one from the "unknown" stack.

2. Present the first known item and have the student read the card aloud.

3. Present the unknown card and read the item aloud (for example, "This is the word 'there.' "), then have the student repeat the word.

4. Tell the student the definition of the unknown word, then have the student repeat the word and its definition.

5. Present the next known card, followed by the unknown. If the student commits an error on any card or hesitates for longer than 2 seconds, the volunteer reads the card aloud, then prompts the student to read it. The rotation between a new known card and the unknown card continues until the student answers all cards within 2 seconds without errors.

6. If the first unknown is now a known, it now replaces a previous known, which is then removed from the stack. Begin the procedure again at Step 4 using a different unknown.

7. Repeat until all unknown cards become known items.

Corrections

None

Adaptations

The Incremental Rehearsal technique can be used with sight or vocabulary words, simple math facts, and letter names and sounds. In addition, this technique could be used for other facts, such as state capitals or the meanings of prefixes or suffixes, etc.

Supported Cloze Procedure
Tier 3 Intervention Strategy
⊙ **TARGETS READING ACCURACY (DECODING) AND COMPREHENSION**

Ms. Cuellar now wants to figure out how to help Julia, an English learner, improve her reading and oral language skills. Based on her curriculum-based assessment scores, she is well below the benchmark in reading fluency. Her score on the state assessment is also well below average. When Ms. Cuellar looks further into Julia's file, she discovers that she is a student with special education needs. She collaborates with Julia's special education teacher to design an instructional plan that will help her succeed.

At the beginning of the year, they look more closely at her reading benchmark assessments and realize that she attempted to read 40 words but only read 30 words correctly. So not only is Julia a dysfluent reader, possibly because of her lack of vocabulary and decoding skills in English, but she is also struggling to read accurately. Together, these challenges significantly affect her ability to comprehend what she is reading in all content areas. Ms. Cuellar and the special education teacher decide to implement the Supported Cloze Procedure (SCP) with a word bank that is previewed before each lesson to activate her prior knowledge of the words and teach academic vocabulary that will be used in context in the strategy (Burns, Riley-Tillman, & VanDerHeyden, 2012).

If possible, the teachers will also provide translation of the vocabulary words for Julia so that she can increase the comprehension of the content as she gains the skills in English. The SCP with the adaptation for this English learner constitutes a Tier 2 or Tier 3 intervention in which a teacher or volunteer reads a passage jointly with a student by reading every other word. In Julia's case, this Tier 2 intervention will happen after she has access to the Tier 1 (core) instruction and ESL supports. The goal of the SCP for Julia includes increasing her decoding skills in English, increasing academic vocabulary related to the English language arts content being taught, and increasing comprehension of the curriculum materials.

Strategy Description

SCP (Burns, Riley-Tillman, & VanDerHeyden, 2012) is a teacher-assisted Tier 2 or Tier 3 intervention in which a teacher or volunteer reads a passage jointly with a student by reading every other word. SCP specifically targets reading accuracy by modeling correct reading of words in the passage. SCP is appropriate for students who have adequate phonetic skills but who struggle applying those skills to reading text.

Recommended Delivery

SCP is an individualized Tier 2 or Tier 3 intervention where the interaction occurs in a student–teacher ratio of 1:1. As a Tier 2 intervention, it should be implemented 3 times per week for at least 20 minutes per session. As a Tier 3 intervention, it should be implemented daily for 15 minutes per session. The strategy occurs between one student and a teacher or volunteer. The student and teacher can sit together at a desk or table. The intervention could occur in a quiet area in the general classroom or in another area of the school, if it makes more sense. You will then want to think about developing a routine for delivering the SCP. This includes:

- establishing a routine for the student to adopt so that he or she knows the step-by-step requirements for engaging in SCP.

- thinking about seating and where materials will be located for SCP.

Facilitator

SCP is teacher-facilitated. A teacher provides feedback as the student reads a passage at his or her instructional level.

Teacher Preparation

Identify an instructional level text. Hi-lo books are recommended for age-appropriate content and are of substantial-enough length to engage in meaningful reading but are not too long so as to overwhelm the students. One-page probes are ideal. You may wish to select a page from the student's hi-lo book so that the student can use material with which he or she is already engaged.

Directions for Implementing

1. Ask the student to orally read the passage while the teacher or volunteer follows along.

2. Any word that the student does not read correctly within 5 seconds is verbally provided by the teacher or volunteer, saying, "That word is _____. What word is that?"

   a. If the student responds correctly, the teacher or volunteer says, "Yes, that word is _____."

   b. If the student responds incorrectly, the teacher or volunteer begins the error correction procedure all over again.

3. After the student reads the passage, the teacher or volunteer says, "This time we are going to read the passage together. Start back at the beginning. You will read the first word. I will read the second, and then we will switch back and forth until we read the whole thing. Any questions?"

4. The student then reads the first word, the teacher or volunteer the second, and so on until the passage is complete. The teacher or volunteer models fluent reading and avoids sounding robotic.

5. Any error by the student is corrected using the error correction procedure described in Step 2.

6. After completing the passage, the pair reads it again. This time, the teacher or volunteer starts with the first word, the student reads the second, and so on. This way, every word on the page is modeled by the teacher or volunteer and read by the student.

Corrections

None

Adaptations

None

Summary

In this chapter, we have introduced and explained six reading strategies that you can use today to begin to improve your students' reading skills. We know that your classrooms are diverse and that you are challenged to meet the needs of struggling learners, ELLs, and students with special education needs. Like Ms. Cuellar, you want a toolkit of strategies that are effective and feasible. You also need strategies that can be used in a variety of formats, like pairs (Partner Reading and Shrink It!), small groups (CSR and Boom!), and teacher- or paraprofessional-led groups (SCP and Incremental Rehearsal).

It is very important that in identifying a strategy presented, you try it yourself first with a student or a peer. You follow the instructions before you teach a volunteer or other adult working with the student. The person should practice with another adult before you send them with the student. It is also crucial to select materials that are age appropriate and engaging. We recommend that you consider hi-lo books as a key choice because they offer age-appropriate content at a variety of reading levels.

By using the instructional delivery models discussed in Chapter 2 and the instructional interventions discussed in this chapter, you are creating a differentiated learning environment that will help your students succeed. In the next chapter, we will describe how to know if your students are responding to the instruction you have in place and what to do if they are not.

CHAPTER 4

Using Hi-Lo Books as Intervention Tools

In Chapter 3, we presented the use of several reading intervention strategies to support students who are struggling in reading, including those with disabilities and ELLs. We identified several features of the intervention strategies as well as instructions for doing them in your classroom. Now that you have learned how to put these intervention strategies into practice, in this chapter we will examine individual case studies of students and look at what type of progress makes sense over time. We will look at the progress of students in reading comprehension by answering the following questions:

- What are the essential components of high-quality Tier 1 (core) instruction?

- What does the classroom data say about your Tier 1 (core) instruction?

- Did your students receive high-quality Tier 1 (core) instruction?

- Does the student in question have the necessary prerequisite skills? If not, what accommodations did you make for him or her to access the core curriculum?

- Is sufficient time devoted to reading fluency practice and vocabulary instruction?

- Is there positive feedback during instruction?

- Did the students receiving reading interventions show growth in reading skills?

- What do you do if the target student is making good progress?

- What do you do if the target student is making slow progress?

- What do you do if the target student is making no progress?

- How can you use hi-lo books to provide strategic instruction and monitor progress?

In Chapter 1, when we presented the research on MTSS, we explained you could expect 75%–85% of your students to be at grade level when your high-quality Tier 1 (core) instruction is actually reaching most of them. This means that based on any assessment or tool that you use, the majority of the students in your classroom are able to access the grade-level reading curriculum or are able to understand the complexity of text and content in the curriculum materials you are presenting to them.

If you are in an urban school district your numbers may look different. In many urban districts, the number of students at grade level can range from 20%–70%. Many schools that have only 20%–40% of students at grade level are usually called turnaround schools or Level 4 schools. This means that these schools have been identified as needing additional resources to rebuild the curriculum and instruction of the school as they increase student outcomes. Most of the turnaround plans incorporate tiered systems of instructional supports, such as MTSS, as part of the very thorough monitoring process. This means that school administrators monitor the Tier 1 (core) instruction and make sure the interventions are supporting student learning.

In Chapter 2, we also introduced you to CBMs, such as oral reading fluency, and how this type of assessment can serve as a universal screener or indicator that tells you when and if interventions can help prevent further lags in reading fluency and comprehension. Remember that CBMs are usually done on an individual basis and take less than 5 minutes to administer. The best approach is to use *all data available*, including CBMs and diagnostic assessments. CBMs are an effective indicator of whether students can read grade-level text. If students cannot read grade-level text, the CBMs indicate that a diagnostic tool may provide the teacher with more detailed information on where the breakdown is happening: decoding and word attack, fluency, comprehension, vocabulary, etc.

Diagnostic assessments are important tools that assess reading comprehension in-depth but take between 30–45 minutes to administer per student. Many schools and districts require that teachers do a universal screener 3 times per year. Sometimes they also require a diagnostic tool 1–3 times per year. Get familiar with your district's policies by asking the following questions:

- What are the tools the school and/or district require?

- What does the school and/or district assess?

- How do I get the results?

- How do parents get the results?

- Is there guidance on how to communicate results of any assessment that is required?

Reading Diagnostic Assessments

Let's take a closer look at how you can look at reading diagnostic assessments. Some examples of diagnostic reading tests you may have seen in your district are the Developmental Reading Assessment (DRA), Scholastic Reading Inventory (SRI), or the Fountas & Pinnell (F&P) Benchmark Assessment System, among many others. For the secondary level, the most commonly used type of diagnostic reading comprehension test results are reported using the Lexile Framework, a theory-based method for measuring the increasing complexity of text. Results, or scores, are reported in Lexiles (White & Clement, 2001).

Lexile scores are part of a framework for reading that is valuable for teachers because it provides a range of where a student's reading ability is, or where the student is before he or she encounters enough difficulty that it impairs their ability to comprehend the content. The Lexile Framework was developed using word and sentence complexity to identify increasing levels of text complexity from Grades K to 12. We refer to this level as instructional versus frustrational. It is critical that we have students working at instructional level when we are teaching new concepts, at independent level when doing independent work or homework, and avoid any frustrational level that can disengage the student from reading for enjoyment and learning. Lexile scores are represented in numbers across grades. The results guide teachers to find books at the student's instructional reading ability, while also providing a way to measure progress over time. This means that if the student is at a particular Lexile level, he or she can comprehend at least 75% of the content read.

Some examples of diagnostic reading comprehension assessments that report Lexile scores are: Progress Toward Standards (PTS3) and the SRI. At the elementary level, reading diagnostic test results provide you either a number or a letter that has an equivalency to a grade-level indicator of reading comprehension. The scores in these assessments are either represented in numbers or letters going from lowest to highest or in alphabetical order, from Grade K to 12.

See Figure 18 for grade-level equivalents of diagnostic test scores. At the elementary level you should ask, how can I make sense of the numbers and letters from diagnostic assessments? At the secondary level you should ask, how can I use information from previous years, and how does it translate to our current Lexile system? The numbers or letters provide information on how students' reading comprehension progresses throughout the year based on complexity of grammar structures, meaning, and vocabulary. In sixth through eighth grade, students move from F&P level U–Z, or from DRA level 70–80, or Lexile level 665L–1165L.

The Lexile Framework

Grade Level Equivalent	Guided Reading Level, Letters (F&P)	Reading Level, Numbers (DRA)	Reading Level, Lexiles
K	AA–C	1–2	BR–70L
1	C–I	3–16	70L–300L
2	J–M	18–28	140L–500L
3	N–P	30–38	330L–700L
4	Q–S	40	445L–810L
5	T–V	50	565L–910L
6	V–Z	50	665L–1000L
7	Z	50	735L–1065L
8	Z	50	805L–1165L
9			855L–1165L
10			905L–1195L
11–12			940L–1210L

BR = beginning reader. Adapted from http://readinga-z.com/readinga-z-levels/level-correlation-chart/ and http://lexile.com/about-lexile/grade-equivalent/grade-equivalent-chart/

FIGURE 18 Grade-Level Equivalents for Diagnostic Test Scores

The benefit of using any one of these approaches is that publishers of curriculum and trade books have categorized their books by Lexile levels, numbers, and/or letters so that you can make better instructional decisions about what are the appropriate books to provide for students who may be below or above grade level. In other words, if you have a sixth grade student reading at an equivalent to third grade reading level or at a Lexile score between 330L–700L, and you would like him to do independent reading, then you would select a book that is within that Lexile level of complexity, and ideally that is age appropriate and of high interest (i.e., hi-lo books in that Lexile score range). Then slowly increase text complexity within the range of 330L–700L, while having the goal to move to the next level as the student improves his or her reading ability and can access books closer to grade-level texts.

Hi-lo books come in a variety of Lexile levels to help you accomplish this range and meet the content- and standards-based requirements. When you are providing direct instruction and guided practice to this student, you would want to increase the grade level and Lexile range by one, (i.e., fourth grade, 445L–810L, which is the student's instructional level. Refer to Figure 18.)

Instructional level means that with direct instruction and teacher facilitation, the student can access more challenging text than if he was reading independently. Knowing the instructional levels of your students helps you plan for accommodations and adaptations for students who may experience grade-level content at a frustrational level.

Frustrational level refers to the point where the student is taking so much time to decode or understand the level of text that comprehension is impaired, and the student is likely to give up. Knowing your students' instructional level and frustrational level (see Figure 19) will help you plan a high-quality Tier 1 (core) lesson.

A Look Inside the Classroom

In Figure 19, Ms. Martinez's seventh grade English language arts classroom in a large urban city, all students were administered the SRI at the beginning of the year.

Student Name	Grade-Level Equivalent	SRI Score	Independent Reading Grade Level	Instructional Reading Grade Level	Frustrational Reading Grade Level
1. Brady	5.0	700L	4.0	5.0	6.0
2. Kim	4.0	445L	3.0	4.0	5.0
3. Sam	5.0	770L	4.0	5.0	6.0
4. David	6.0	735L	5.0	6.0	7.0
5. Isabella	7.0	1065L	6.0	7.0	8.0
6. Donna	6.0	900L	5.0	6.0	7.0
7. Evan	4.0	450L	3.0	4.0	5.0
8. Erica	5.0	600L	4.0	5.0	6.0
9. Diana	5.0	600L	4.0	5.0	6.0
10. Ana	5.0	500L	4.0	5.0	6.0
11. Ronald	7.0	1000L	4.0	5.0	6.0
12. Jack	7.0	990L	4.0	5.0	6.0
13. Benjamin	9.0	1195L	4.0	5.0	6.0
14. Charlotte	5.0	600L	4.0	5.0	6.0
15. Ravi	7.0	880L	5.0	6.0	7.0
16. Mark	3.0	430L	2.0	3.0	4.0
17. Annalisse	3.0	650L	2.0	3.0	4.0
18. Wen	7.0	800L	6.0	7.0	8.0
19. Song	6.0	900L	5.0	6.0	7.0
20. John	5.0	565L	4.0	5.0	6.0
21. Rom	5.0	600L	4.0	5.0	6.0
22. Efrain	9.0	1200L	4.0	5.0	6.0
23. Gabriel (Newcomer. ELL.)	1.0	300L	No English	No English	No English

FIGURE 19 Ms. Martinez's Seventh Grade Reading Comprehension Results, Beginning of Year Analysis

The breakdown of Ms. Martinez's seventh grade class is as follows:

- 8/23 students or 34.5% of her students are at the equivalent to fifth grade level.

- 5/23 students or 22% of her students are at the equivalent to seventh grade level.

- 5/23 students or 22% of her students are more than three grade levels below, including one newcomer with no English language.

- 3/23 students or 13% of her students are one grade below.

- 2/23 students or 8.5% of her students are above grade level, with both students reading two grade levels above seventh grade.

Based on this initial assessment of where students are on this measure of comprehension, Ms. Martinez can assume that for the present until January (or middle of the year reassessment) that less than one-third of her students will benefit from her grade-level instruction. This means that Ms. Martinez needs to think differently about her lesson plans and instructional delivery. Differentiated instruction, preventive Tier 2 interventions (i.e., strategic and additional), and Tier 3 interventions (i.e., intensive and additional) to meet the needs of the students are going to be a part of her new planning. She needs to think about how to provide access to the seventh grade curriculum to all her students, including those who are just one grade level behind, all the way to the new ELL in her class.

Knowing how important high-quality Tier 1 (core) instruction is, Ms. Martinez will develop lessons plans with differentiation for all students, accounting for the variety of reading levels. Then she will also plan for the five students reading significantly below grade level for additional Tier 2 and Tier 3 interventions that will help the students reach grade-level content.

Instructional Interventions Inside the Classroom

Let's look back at how Ms. Martinez can support a variety of learners in her class by using effective instructional interventions for the students with below grade-level reading comprehension skills.

Annalisse and Mark are reading at the equivalent to a third grade instructional reading level. This means that they will experience difficulty decoding seventh grade reading materials. It may slow them down enough to impact comprehension skills. They will also need more time to complete the work. A preview lesson with a word bank may help them learn the vocabulary associated with the lesson ahead of time. For independent work, Ms. Martinez must select materials that follow the content of the lesson but that are written at lower reading levels. Hi-lo books are a perfect resource to support Tier 1 (core) instruction. For example, if the students are reading fantasy as a class, then during independent reading, the students would have the option to select novels of the same genre written at lower Lexile levels.

Kim and Ethan, who are reading at the equivalent to a fourth grade instructional reading level, or around a 450L, may experience difficulty decoding seventh grade reading materials. It may slow them down enough to impact comprehension skills. They may also need more time to complete the work and may benefit from having peer-mediated reading time with a student who is reading at grade level. They may also benefit from vocabulary practice in small groups and more strategies for word attack with fourth and fifth grade reading words. For independent work, Ms. Martinez must select materials that follow the content of the lesson but that are written at lower reading levels. A perfect resource to support Tier 1 (core) instruction are hi-lo books. For example, if in Ms. Martinez's seventh grade classroom they are reading nonfiction biographies, then during independent reading, the students would have the option to select biographies that relate to the curriculum but are written at lower Lexile levels.

Ethan is a student with special education needs. He has a learning disability. Ms. Martinez will coordinate with the special education teacher for services in the IEP, and she will also plan Tier 1 (core) and Tier 2 small-group interventions. She and the special education teacher may find that using a graphic organizer during reading will provide Ethan with the structure he needs to organize the sequence, main characters, climax, and conclusion in the books the class is reading.

For Gabriel, the student who is an ELL and newcomer with limited English, Ms. Martinez can also select fantasy and graphic novels or audiobooks from lower-level hi-lo titles that have enough pictures and action to scaffold the student's understanding of the story. She can further provide a word bank that links to cognates of the primary language of the student if available (see http://www.colorincolorado.org/educators/background/cognates/).

Cognates are words in two languages that share a similar meaning, spelling, and pronunciation (Colorín Colorado, 2007). Thirty percent to 40% of words in Spanish have a related word in English. Additionally, Ms. Martinez can also collaborate with the ESL teacher. She can share the genre being addressed in the curriculum and list key vocabulary words that will appear in the text Gabriel is reading as part of the ESL support in Tier 1 (core) instruction.

Ms. Martinez is now ready to follow and teach the curriculum standards in seventh grade with differentiated instruction and strategies to support the students in her class who will need Tier 2 and perhaps even Tier 3 intervention in addition to her own high-quality Tier 1 (core) instruction.

Components of an Intervention

As a reminder to the expectation of what Tier 2 constitutes, students below grade level will receive additional intervention in the area of comprehension and word attack skills in small groups of 4–6 students for at least 20 minutes, 3 times per week.

The teacher or interventionist will provide evidence through a checklist (fidelity check) that the students did receive small-group instruction for the time identified as part of a Tier 2 intervention in addition to Tier 1 (core) and ESL support (if needed).

If the students have a disability, they would receive their specialized instruction according to their IEP in addition to the Tier 1 (core) instruction Ms. Martinez is delivering *plus* Tier 2 small-group instruction.

Monthly progress monitoring using CBMs is expected and should be part of the intervention activities. The information is used to monitor that students are benefitting or making progress as a result of instruction and intervention.

A Look Inside the Classroom

Now that Ms. Martinez has a baseline for the entire class in terms of both reading level and specific skills, she will reassess all students in the middle of the year and then again at the end of the year. This is important because if the percentages change, Ms. Martinez will need to make instructional decisions about how to better meet the needs of her students. Let's move to Figure 20 and examine a middle of the year progress report in Ms. Martinez's class.

Student Name	Score Grade-Level Equivalent Fall CBM (ORF)	Score Fall SRI (BM)	Score Grade-Level Equivalent Winter CBM (ORF)	Score Winter SRI (BM)	Score Grade-Level Equivalent Spring CBM (ORF)	Score Spring F&P (BM)
1. Brady	5.0/95	700L	6.5/100	880L*		
2. Kim	4.0/74	445L	4.5/102	550L*		
3. Sam	5.0/100	770L	5.5/110	860L*		
4. David	6.0/110	735L	6.0/115	785L		
5. Isabella	7.0/110	1065L	7.5/114	1100L*		
6. Donna	6.0/100	900L	6.5/118	980L*		
7. Evan	4.0/74	450L	4.5/120	450L*		
8. Erica	5.0/95	600L	5.0/101	660L		
9. Diana	5.0/94	600L	5.0/99	650L		
10. Ana	5.0/93	500L	5.5/109	680L*		
11. Ronald	5.0/101	1000L	5.0/113	1100L		
12. Jack	7.0/97	990L	7.5/117	1150L*		
13. Benjamin	9.0/99	1195L	9.0/106	1180L		
14. Charlotte	5.0/99	600L	5.5/112	660L*		
15. Ravi	7.0/119	880L	7.5/129	950L*		
16. Mark	3.0/45	430L	3.5/56	500L*		
17. Annalisse	3.0/70	650L	3.5/100	800L*		
18. Wen	7.0/129	800L	7.0/132	800L		
19. Song	6.0/110	900L	6.0/115	910L		
20. John	5.0/100	565L	5.5/110	580L*		
21. Rom	5.0/99	600L	5.5/114	660L*		

Table continued on p. 77

Student Name	Score Grade-Level Equivalent Fall CBM (ORF)	Score Fall BM SRI	Score Grade-Level Equivalent Winter CBM (ORF)	Score Winter BM SRI	Score Grade-Level Equivalent Spring CBM (ORF)	Score Spring BM F&P
22. Efrain	9.0/91	1200L	9.5/106	1210L*		
23. Gabriel (Newcomer. ELL.)	1.0/10	300L	3.0/30	350L*		

ORF = oral reading fluency; BM = benchmark average. *Indicates students moved up in reading level.

FIGURE 20 Ms. Martinez's Seventh Grade Reading Comprehension Results, Beginning to Middle of Year

As you take a look at Figure 20, the students with an asterisk are those who moved up in reading level or within range of a Lexile change across one grade to another on the SRI. In other words, 70% made at least a half-grade level of progress, as expected, for this time of the year. This suggests that Ms. Martinez's reading instruction is supporting most of her learners, or the expected number of students have enough access to the content to make a half-year's growth.

Ms. Martinez also had students who didn't make progress, as evidenced by the CBM, the grade-level equivalent, and SRI. Three students reading two levels behind, two students reading slightly below level, one student at grade level, and one student reading above grade level did not make progress. This suggests that these students may be struggling.

For those reading one and two grade levels behind and who are receiving Tier 2 and perhaps even Tier 3 support, Ms. Martinez will have to further investigate if the intervention has been delivered as intended and if they need to add, change, or increase the intervention.

For students making progress, Ms. Martinez should continue to do what she's doing—it's working! And for students at grade level and above, Ms. Martinez needs to reevaluate her Tier 1 (core) reading instruction to see how she can ensure that all students at the end of the year are making progress. Some of the strategies she can define more specifically for this purpose are:

- She could adopt the Partner Reading strategy discussed in Chapter 3 and ensure that all students are reading books at their instructional level and are giving each other corrective feedback as part of the process. She should ensure that this happens at least 3 times per week for 20 minutes in her class.

- She could also have students begin to monitor themselves using a 1-minute CBM probe from their peer reading folder. Ms. Martinez would have to introduce how to do the strategy and give each student a graph where they can begin to monitor their own progress twice per month.

- She can reevaluate how much time her students are actively engaged in reading activities. And she can increase opportunities for students at and above grade level to demonstrate strategies to increase their comprehension, such as asking the students to make predictions, identify the main idea, and support the main idea citing areas of the text as different levels of text complexity are presented.

While Ms. Martinez reevaluates her Tier 1 (core) reading instruction, she should also begin to monitor the individual progress of each of the students reading below grade level to further understand the unique progress they are making, or what is called the "rate of learning." In order to do that, Ms. Martinez will collect information from Tier 2 and Tier 3 interventions and develop a growth chart based on oral reading fluency norms for each of the students on the progress-monitoring CBM probes she has been collecting (at least) monthly. Let's take a closer look at Evan and Kim, who are both reading three reading levels behind. Kim has made Lexile level progress, but Evan has not.

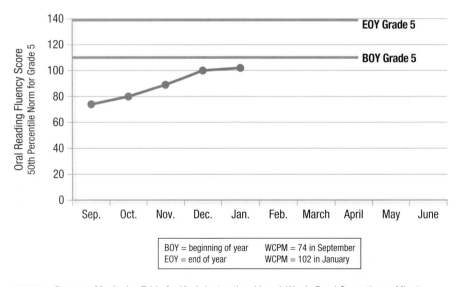

FIGURE 21 Progress Monitoring Table for Kim's Instructional Level, Words Read Correctly per Minute

Progress Monitoring Inside the Classroom

Let's take a look at Kim's CBM progress monitoring words read correctly per minute from September to January in Figure 21. Remember that CBMs provide an indication of how the student is making progress in fluency, which is highly correlated to reading comprehension. This means that if the CBM score is increasing, so should the reading Lexile level. Please note that although Kim is in seventh grade, the progress monitoring activities at her instructional level provide the teacher with rich information, including that the intervention activities designed for Kim are working. This should be one aspect of progress monitoring, but the teacher should also note that Kim is making progress and growing, even if the growth is below grade-level expectations. All students must be taught where they are (i.e., at their instructional level).

As you can see from the progress monitoring growth in the fluency skills graph, Kim is making nice progress, but in the middle of the year, she is still at the equivalent to fifth grade as a seventh grader. There is also the potential that her progress is leveling off as you look at December and January. Ms. Martinez should ask the following questions:

- Is the intervention happening as scheduled or intended?

- Does the intervention focus on reading practice or fluency?

- Does the teacher providing the intervention feel that word attack skills using fifth grade reading level materials are slowing Kim down and impairing her comprehension?

- If the intervention is 3 times per week for 20 minutes, can additional time or one more day be added? If so, what activities or strategies should she focus on that day?

- Should the teacher providing Tier 2 interventions evaluate if the student should continue using hi-lo books as part of the strategy to build fluency and comprehension? If the student is still at a fourth grade reading level, Ms. Martinez should consider continuing the use of hi-lo books until a greater rate of growth is evident in the data.

Let's take a look at Evan in Figure 22. Evan started the year reading at the same level and skill as Kim in the CBM. However, he has not increased reading fluency, and he is still at the same Lexile level.

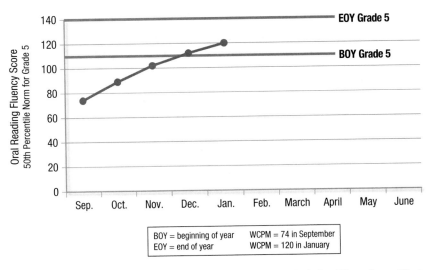

FIGURE 22 Progress Monitoring Table for Evan's Instructional Level, Words Read Correctly per Minute

Evan's growth chart demonstrates a different learning path. Evan is showing steady progress from 74 words read correctly in 1 minute in September to 120 words read correctly in the middle of the year. From his growth, Ms. Martinez can expect that Evan will meet grade-level expectation in his ability to read seventh grade content fluently, but there is still a question about reading comprehension and why it's not improving at the same rate as fluency. Here are some questions she should consider as she plans the rest of the year:

- Should Ms. Martinez continue, decrease, or increase the frequency and intensity of the Tier 2 intervention each week moving forward from January to June?

- If there are 30 weeks of school, and average expected growth in reading fluency skills is one word per week, how do you know if he will make the end of year expectation? (Fifteen weeks = 15 words. If he started at 74 words per minute, he should be at 90 words per minute. He has reached 120 words per minute, which is twice the level of growth expected). Evaluate the intervention Evan is receiving and see if other students can benefit from it.

- Has Evan's progress in fluency also affected comprehension? He started at a Lexile level of 450L and scored the same in the middle of the year. His fluency gains are not impacting or translating into reading comprehension growth. Ms. Martinez needs to go back to the IEP. Was reading fluency the right intervention for Evan? Would he benefit from having an intervention that focused on comprehension skills instead? Should it be both?

- Has the teacher working with Evan in the Tier 2 intervention updated materials to represent equivalent to fifth grade level complexity? Was the student able to respond? If so, re-administer the SRI or use another diagnostic tool to learn more about Evan's specific reading skills.

- In Ms. Martinez's Tier 1 (core) instruction, has she updated the small-group and large-group instructional activities so that Evan has a greater opportunity to interact with and be challenged by kids at his grade level?

Now, let's refer back to Figure 20 and take a look at students who are two grade levels behind. Annalisse and Mark's data demonstrate that they are at an instructional third grade reading level in reading comprehension. Looking more closely at the SRI Lexile score, Annalisse is reading at the equivalent of a middle-of-the-year third grade level, with a CBM oral reading fluency score of 70 words read correctly in 1 minute.

Mark, who is an ELL Level 3, is reading at the equivalent of a beginning third grade level, with a CBM oral reading fluency score of 45 words read correctly in 1 minute. For these two students, Ms. Martinez should be providing Tier 2 and Tier 3 interventions in addition to high-quality Tier 1 (core) instruction. This means that Ms. Martinez and her colleagues must *ensure* that after core instruction is provided with ESL supports for Mark, each of them also gets small-group instruction for at least 20 minutes, 3 times per week, and individualized instruction another 30 minutes per week, tailored to their particular area of reading difficulty (phonemic awareness, phonics, fluency, comprehension, and/or vocabulary).

For Annalisse, one good option is to use hi-lo books at an instructional third grade reading level. While for Mark, Ms. Martinez should select hi-lo books at an instructional second grade reading level. For example, if the class is reading *Dracula*, she can provide access to hi-lo books during small-group instruction and independent practice in order for the student to be able to follow the class discussions and activities. In addition, the intervention should use the vocabulary and cloze reading activities described in the book and monitor progress weekly. Once students are progressing in fluency and accuracy, then Ms. Martinez and her colleagues can move up the different levels of hi-lo curriculum materials for *Dracula*. Hi-lo books for *Dracula* can be found in a range of Lexile levels.

Keep in mind the idea is for students to be making progress so that you can increase the level of complexity of the texts, while also allowing students to be easily engaged with the topic of discussion in the classroom and the theme identified in the curriculum.

Let's take a closer look at what happened to Annalisse and Mark during the 5-month period of September to January. What instructional and intervention decisions should Ms. Martinez make in the middle of the school year? As you see in each case study, here are specific questions to think about:

- Are Annalisse and Mark receiving a high-quality Tier 1 (core) instruction?

- Are Annalisse and Mark receiving Tier 2 intervention in small-group instruction at least 3 times per week for 20 minutes?

- Is the Tier 2 intervention showing impact on fluency growth on bi-monthly progress monitoring checks?

- If there is no sign of progress on the progress monitoring checks, will the intervention be increased in frequency (times per week), duration (extended time per session), or intensity (more specialized approaches)? Should the intervention(s) address all the areas of literacy or just one for each student (i.e., phonemic awareness, decoding, vocabulary, fluency, comprehension, and oral language development).

Let's take a look at Annalisse's CBM progress monitoring from September to January in Figure 23.

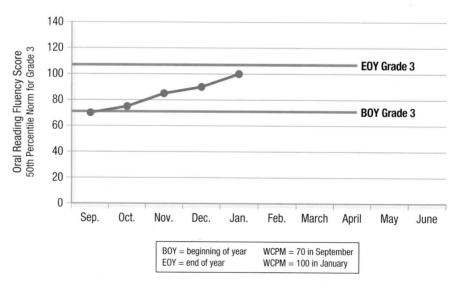

FIGURE 23 Progress Monitoring Table for Annalisse's Instructional Level, Words Read Correctly per Minute

Annalisse's growth chart demonstrates steady progress from 74 words read correctly in 1 minute (or oral reading fluency) in September to 100 words read correctly in the middle of the year. From this pattern, Ms. Martinez can expect that Annalisse will be very close to meeting equivalent to end of fifth grade oral reading fluency expectation, which suggests that she will be able to read content written at the equivalent of fifth grade by the end of the school year.

This represents a two-grade equivalent growth level, with a good plan for summer support to potentially reach seventh grade-level content. Because of the growth, Ms. Martinez should continue the instruction and intervention plan she has developed for Annalisse. She should continue to monitor monthly and begin increasing the complexity of text, moving from hi-lo books written at a third grade reading level to a fourth and fifth grade reading level, with a plan to start slowly increasing exposure to grade-level content during intervention time.

Mark's growth chart in Figure 24 demonstrates an initial progress from 43 words read correctly in 1 minute (or oral reading fluency) in September to 69 words read correctly in November, and then a sudden decrease mid-year. Ms. Martinez should address the following questions:

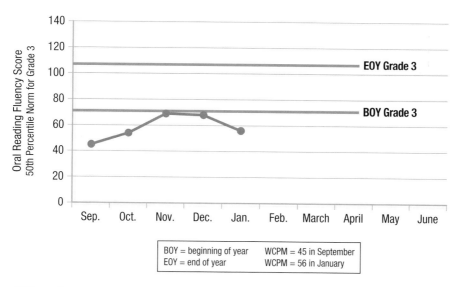

FIGURE 24 Progress Monitoring Table for Mark's Instructional Level, Words Read Correctly per Minute

- Did Mark have access to high-quality Tier 1 (core) instruction in her classroom?

- Is Mark's IEP being delivered with fidelity? If so, what special education services should he be receiving in addition to Tier 1 (core) and Tier 2, and how does this coordinate with and support the other?

- Is the student an ELL? If so, is the student receiving ESL services by a certified ESL teacher? Should information on the student's first language be explored for literacy skills in that language and language(s) spoken at home?

- Have all teachers working with the student met to monitor all the instructional, intervention, and specialized services?

- Did Mark demonstrate academic engagement during class?

- How many days was Mark absent during the time from September to November and from November to January?

- How many days was Mark present for Tier 2 interventions? Was the teacher assigned to work with Mark on the Tier 2 intervention there to do it?

- What current materials are being used in the interventions?

- What strategies are being used with the materials?

- Is the student in a small group and is he actively engaged?

- Was the intervention delivered with fidelity?

- Can the team of teachers working with Ms. Martinez meet and create a new plan of instruction and intervention? What will be different? What will be the same? What additional materials and/or resources will they need?

Once this information is collected, Ms. Martinez and her colleagues can develop a new plan for the second half of the year. The information gathered is a good way to ensure that the teachers don't continue to provide the same level of supports that were not working, assuming that the student is attending school. This kind of data-driven collaborative planning also allows for existing supports, which didn't work for some students. However, these existing supports may be allocated to other students in her classroom, who may benefit from the intervention.

English Learners Inside the Classroom

Finally, let's take a look at Gabriel. Gabriel is new at the school and is an English learner. As a new seventh grader with Level 2 English skills, this means that Gabriel has a few English words, mostly used during interpersonal exchanges with his peers. He is beginning to interact orally with other students, but decoding, syntax (i.e., sentence structure), and semantics, or vocabulary, is highly limited. Gabriel should be receiving support from the ESL teacher for 2 hours per day in the regular education classroom or in a pull-out placement. The ESL teacher should be working on using the grade-level materials to provide direct instruction on vocabulary, word attack skills, and interpersonal language.

Typically, English learners are assessed in four main areas: listening, speaking, reading, and writing. Each of these areas is measured in five levels, typically described as Proficiency Level 1, which describes Beginning Level to Level 5 or 6, which represents fluency in interpersonal and academic language approaching those of native language speakers. It is important to note that just because students reach a Level 5 or 6 proficiency, it does not mean there will not be differences in the abilities in the four areas.

For example, an English learner living in the U.S. for 30 years may still have an accent and may still use conventions of language that are not 100% correct. Native language learned in the formative years, 0–8 years old, impact all levels of information and formal language. Students new to the English language will typically go through several stages of oral language development that mirror the language development of children. They will begin by using simple nouns and adjectives, and quickly increase their ability to grow in complexity with sentence structure, fluency in the four areas, and vocabulary.

What teachers should note is that students need to increase their oral and academic language proficiency. There are many measures provided by the research, the state, and even districts that can give you markers of where students are increasing proficiency as their time in the U.S. grows. According to the research on oral language development, it takes 5–8 years to learn the interpersonal (or oral language) and academic language in a second language. This means that if a 10-year-old student is a new English learner in your fifth grade classroom and has limited oral proficiency skills in English (describing him as being a Level 1), then it will take until he is at least 15 years old, or in tenth grade, to approach interpersonal and academic proficiency in the English language. During this time, these students have had the double burden of learning the academic curriculum expected at their grade as well as increasing their skills and language proficiency in a second language. As a result, here are some recommendations to adopt in your classrooms:

- Learn who your English learners are and where they are in their levels of oral language proficiency in each of the four areas: listening, speaking, reading, and writing.

- Acknowledge that having two languages is an asset and beneficial, and that their culture is important in your classrooms. Provide opportunities for students to share how similar things are done in their countries.

- Try to learn their language and encourage students to do so as well.

- Use this information to differentiate instruction and apply interventions in your classroom. For example, labeling typical items in your classroom is helpful for all students. Create word banks of content vocabulary that will be used regularly, and pair it with visuals made by students.

- When developing interventions, identify texts that will relate to the student's prior experiences or knowledge and that potentially embrace their culture.

- Monitor monthly the gains that they are making in each of the areas using a checklist.

Now, let's go back Gabriel. As noted, he has been in the U.S. for just two years. He speaks Cape Verdean and can read and write in his language according to his family. He has two siblings at home, and he helps them with their homework. He loves basketball and seems interested in graphic novels. He is attentive in class and loves science and math. His writing is limited in sentence structure and complexity. He also is shy to read aloud or answer questions in class. He sometimes daydreams but is easily redirected. Ms. Martinez has been required to do CBM or measures of oral reading fluency for all her students including Gabriel as seen in Figure 25. However, Ms. Martinez has also been collecting a summary of skills in listening, speaking, reading, and writing that she has observed to have increased over this school year.

From the monthly "Progress Monitoring for English Language Learners Checklist" that Ms. Martinez developed, as seen in Figure 26, she can see the new skills that Gabriel has been demonstrating from September through December.

She is pleased to see that Gabriel is willing to now answer simple questions in class. Ms. Martinez will ensure that she develops an opportunity for him to answer simple questions daily, moving from *yes* and *no* questions to

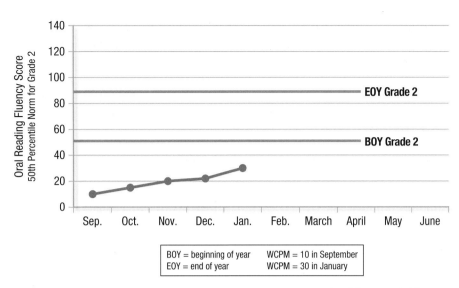

BOY = beginning of year   WCPM = 10 in September
EOY = end of year   WCPM = 30 in January

FIGURE 25 Progress Monitoring Table for Gabriel's Instructional Level, Words Read Correctly per Minute

more *how, when, why, what,* and *who* questions over the rest of the school year, using hi-lo books at a second or third grade reading level. This level of questioning will also be a focus in the Tier 2 small-group intervention in order to increase vocabulary and grammar structure.

"Progress Monitoring for English Language Learners" Checklist

NAME: ___GABRIEL___

Proficiency Indicators for Listening Level 1 (L1), Level 2 (L2), Level 3 (L3)	September	October	November	December
L1 Comprehension of a few words, phrases, with basic English grammatical forms		X	X	X
L1 Focus attention selective during new concepts in the classroom		X	X	X
L1 Listens to and imitates others' use of language	X	X	X	X
L2 Discriminates sounds and information patterns of the English language				X
L2 Follows multi-steps oral directives to complete a task			X	X
L2 Understands basic structures, expressions, and vocabulary, such as school environments and basic personal information (e.g., home, address, emergency number)			X	X
			(*X* means behavior is evident in observation)	

Table continued on p. 88

Proficiency Indicators for Listening Level 1 (L1), Level 2 (L2), Level 3 (L3)	September	October	November	December
L3 Listens attentively to stories/information and identifies main idea, key details, and concepts using both verbal and non-verbal cues of the speaker			X	X

Proficiency Indicators for Speaking Level 1 (L1), Level 2 (L2), Level 3 (L3)	September	October	November	December
S1 Names people, places, objects, events, and basic concepts, such as days of the week, food, occupations, and time		X	X	X
S1 Answers questions with one- or two-word responses		X	X	X
S1 Generates a few words and phrases with basic English grammatical form and phonemic accuracy			X	X
S1 Communicates basic needs, wants, and feelings		X	X	X
S2 Restates oral directions or instructions			X	X
S2 Asks and answers questions using simple phrases and sentences				X
S2 Narrates basic sequence of events				X
S3 Converses in simple topics, beginning to use most conventions of oral language, including intonation, syntax, and grammar (subject-verb agreement)				X
S3 Prepares and delivers short oral presentations (tells a story using pictures on an academic topic)				

Proficiency Indicators for Reading Level 1 (L1), Level 2 (L2), Level 3 (L3)				
R1 Identifies words from left to right and upright position	X	X	X	X
R1 Recognizes the alphabet, Arabic numbers, and begins to recognize sounds	X	X	X	X
R1 Reads simple one-syllable and high-frequency words when strongly supported by context	X	X	X	X
R2 Recognizes sounds/symbol relationships and sounds of the English language		X	X	X
R2 Uses cognates for academic or social comprehension				X
R2 Reads common word families and simple sentences			X	X
R3 Locates meaning, pronunciations, and derivations of unfamiliar words using dictionaries, glossaries, or Internet				X
R3 Recognizes and uses knowledge of spelling patterns when reading				X
R3 Identifies main idea				

(*X* means behavior is evident in observation)

Table continued on p. 89

Proficiency Indicators for Writing Level 1 (L1), Level 2 (L2), Level 3 (L3)				
W1 Prints legibly for age using left to right, top to bottom directionality	X	X	X	X
W1 Copies words posted and commonly used in the classroom	X	X	X	X
W1 Capitalizes first words of a sentence, proper nouns, and initials (e.g., names, months, etc.)		X	X	X
W2 Uses phonetic spelling			X	X
W2 Fills out simple forms with personal information			X	X
W2 Begins to demonstrate knowledge of paragraphs structure				X
W3 Begins to convey conventional spelling				
W3 Identifies complete and incomplete sentences is writing in English				
W3 Writes friendly notes and letters				X
W3 Begins to edit writing for punctuation, capitalization, and spelling				

(*X* means behavior is evident in observation)

Based on an adapted version Ms. Martinez created from http://www.bogalusaschools.org

FIGURE 26 Ms. Martinez's "Progress Monitoring for English Language Learners" Checklist

Ms. Martinez is also excited that Gabriel is now beginning to share notes with peers and seems to be copying from the whiteboard with a high degree of accuracy as he begins to understand the decoding and grammatical structures of the English language. In summary, Ms. Martinez is pleased that Gabriel is demonstrating some of the indicators of Level 3 skills in all areas: listening, speaking, reading, and writing. She will continue to provide the same level of Tier 1 (core), ESL, and Tier 2 interventions despite the fact that his oral reading fluency is showing very slow progress. She also knows that in January she will provide Gabriel with the F&P Benchmark Assessment System to see what his reading comprehension level is with grade-level materials.

In this chapter, we provided an in-depth analysis of the instructional histories of a complete seventh grade language arts class. We then followed five students performing below grade level. We provided you with questions to guide your instructional planning and intervention processes and described how hi-lo books can be used to support students' learning. We further explained how you can look at data 3 times a year for all students and monthly for the students below grade level. We presented how to monitor students' progress and make predictions about whether students will approach grade-level or end-of-year expected benchmarks. We provided you with questions to consider if students are not on track, and how to know when to change an intervention approach to make it more effective.

In the Appendix, you will find blank copies of the informal assessment tools ("Reading Instruction" Teacher Self-Assessment) and questioning guides (Common Planning Time: Asking Questions of Your Data) that you can take with you when you meet with your colleagues.

We hope that you were able to identify your own students and classroom challenges in the examples we provided. Using hi-lo books to provide students with grade-level curriculum topics and independent and instructional reading opportunities, we feel confident that you will increase your students' engagement with the subject. What we do know is that when students are engaged, they learn! Always evaluate how you can organize and plan instruction that actively engages students, regardless of whether they are students with disabilities or students learning English, because creating multi-tiered structures that provide preventive intervention will help them reach higher levels of active engagement and stronger educational outcomes.

In Chapter 5, we conclude this book by providing ways to monitor your own high-quality Tier 1 (core) instruction to ensure that it is differentiated, engaging, and balanced, and to ensure that it meets the needs of most students in your class.

CHAPTER 5

Common Pitfalls of MTSS

In Chapter 3, we presented some reading intervention strategies to support students who are struggling in reading, including those with disabilities or who are learning English. We identified several features of the intervention strategies as well as "how tos" for doing them in your classroom. In Chapter 4, we reviewed how much progress to expect over time. Now that you have learned how to intervene and what kind of progress to expect, this chapter will present how you can ensure that students are benefiting from the Tier 1 (core) instruction and the reading intervention strategies.

High-Quality Instruction

During their training programs, teachers are always told that an effective lesson should include an evaluation component. More often than not as we teach, we run out of time, and we don't get to check for understanding or to conduct an evaluation of the objective of the lesson. It is critical that as you develop Tier 1 (core) lessons, you take an opportunity to ensure that you do check for understanding. Most importantly, after each lesson, you must reflect on its effectiveness and quality. Here are some questions to ask yourself about your high-quality instruction:

- Did you present the lesson's objective?

- Did the students know the lesson's objective? (Did the lesson's objective meet the discrete areas of reading skills and instruction?)

- Did you activate the students' prior knowledge about the lesson's topic?

- Were the students—in small groups, large groups, pairs, or independent—actively engaged in the lesson's topic?

- Did you teach the objective and skill as intended? If not, consider what got in your way of doing what you intended.

- Did you provide guided practice that included modeling of the skills (e.g., decoding skills, fluency practice, vocabulary use, or comprehension questions)?

- Did you provide students with an opportunity for independent practice as individuals or as part of a pair or group?

- Did you bring the students back at the end of the lesson to review the content learned and evaluate how well they understood the concept?
- Did you take time to think about what went well in the lesson and what did not?

The Lesson's Objective

Let's begin by addressing each of these questions step-by-step to ensure that you have provided a high-quality Tier 1 (core) instructional lesson and delivery. Once we can be assured that you have effectively delivered a standards-based core lesson, then we can look at the specific progress of each student. And we can consider which tools to use to ensure that the intervention time and strategy is effective and efficient. First, did you present the lesson's objective? And did the students know the lesson's objective? (Did the lesson's objective meet the discrete area of reading skills and instruction?)

As you think about lesson's objective, it is critical to look at CCSS and your state standards, if your state has not adopted CCSS. Standards guide districts and schools in what should be taught in each curriculum area and in each grade. As you develop the lessons, you can use your reading or English language arts curriculum materials and cross-check that the lesson's objective match one of the CCSS or state standards, or you can begin with CCSS or state standards and find the content in your curriculum materials or scope and sequence of your curriculum maps. Either approach is effective.

Common Planning Time

The most effective approach, however, is to use the structure or the time that your school provides, sometimes called Common Planning Time, to go over which standards you and your grade-level colleagues will be addressing in order to build greater consistency and delivery of a strong core instruction.

Not too long ago, teachers would typically teach in their classroom and were not given time to plan with each other. Most of the time, teachers did not even know what was happening in the classroom next door, that, perhaps, taught students of the same grade. In fact, you may still be teaching in a school that has this practice. If so, we encourage you to find the other colleagues in your grade and get together to plan.

Working with other colleagues offers several advantages that result in a stronger and more consistent approach to Tier 1 (core) instruction. All teachers in the grade-level team benefit from the teaching experience you each bring to the table. All teachers in the grade-level team are trained in a particular area of education and by different experts, so the "cross-training" enhances the teaching practices you currently use. All teachers in the grade level-team can compare the progress that students are making across different classrooms and talk about how teachers are using different ways or strategies to teach different concepts. All teachers in the grade-level team can adopt innovative ways to share with students across the grade so that students can get the benefit from the most trained or experienced teachers (e.g., struggling students getting intervention strategies from the most experienced teacher).

Activate Prior Knowledge

Once you have identified the standards-based objectives for your lessons, the next goal is to introduce the lesson by activating the students' prior knowledge. Activation of prior knowledge involves getting students to think about anything that relates to the topic based on their personal experiences. In a typical lesson about a new book, a picture walk or a book cover discussion can be very effective in engaging the students to think about what they know that relates to the topic. A picture walk or a book cover discussion refers to having the students taking a look at the interior pictures or front cover of the book. If the book, such as a graphic novel, has many pictures, ask the students to browse through the pictures for a few minutes and then share with their peers what they think the story is about, what it reminds them of, and any questions they may have.

At this point, it is very effective and a recommended practice for the teacher to introduce new vocabulary by letting students use the Frayer Method. The Frayer Method (Frayer, Frederick and Klausmejer, 1969) has been a very effective, long-standing strategy to support students' vocabulary development using a graphic organizer. Students get a worksheet that is broken into four sections. Each section addresses a different activity about the new vocabulary word that students, in pairs or small groups, complete. The key aspect of the strategy requires that the student uses his or her own words to describe and define the word and provide an example and a non-example (see Figure 27).

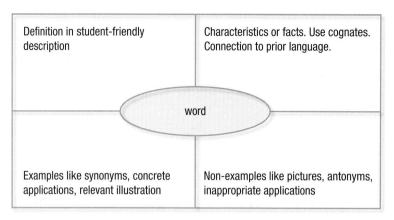

FIGURE 27 The Frayer Method

Once you address vocabulary, the lesson must also identify how you will teach the rest: word attack and decoding, fluency and accuracy of reading, and comprehension. Once you complete the teaching of each skill area within your lesson, make sure that you take some time and complete a short fidelity checklist, as in Figure 28, that reviews whether you were able to deliver the instruction in each of the areas of reading that you intended to teach.

Literacy Skills

Phonemic Awareness: identifying sounds (phonemes) in spoken words
Word Attack: decoding words in connected text linking the ability to read isolated sounds to new words
Fluency: reading a text quickly and with accuracy
Vocabulary: understanding words to get meaning and to convey meaning
Comprehension: understanding the meaning of a text in connected text

In each box, note the *number of minutes* you teach the above literacy skills to your whole group.

Days of Week/Reading Skill	Monday	Tuesday	Wednesday	Thursday	Friday	Daily Average
Phonemic Awareness						
Work Attack						
Fluency						
Vocabulary						
Comprehension						

FIGURE 28 Fidelity Checklist

Student Engagement

The next set of questions address the area of student engagement. If students are actively engaged, they learn. It is critical to reflect on how your Tier 1 (core) instructional lesson plan addresses student engagement. It is easy to become lecturers in our classrooms, so it is important to incorporate a variety of multi-modal instructional formats or universally designed formats during your teaching. Lecturing is the way most of us were taught. But based on research, we now know that breaking the period into smaller chunks of time and engaging students in a variety of ways provides for higher student engagement and yields more evidence of learning.

In delivering your lesson, did you break it into chunks of 10–20 minutes? Did the activities vary from whole-class instruction (e.g., a large-group picture walk or book cover discussion, introducing new vocabulary, a mini-lesson on a comprehension strategy)? Any method for delivery of instruction, including whole-class instruction, should last no more than 10–20 minutes. In fact, many schools recommend that teachers use mini-lessons to teach new concepts. A mini-lesson is a 12–17 minute instructional delivery model where the teacher can focus the whole class on a particular area of

FIGURE 29 Whole Class Mini-Lesson

discussion, exploration, or demonstration that will inform the rest of the lesson. Once we can consistently run a mini-lesson based on the time limitation and the content, we can successfully provide the first part of the lesson in whole-group format.

Small-Group Instruction

Next, did you think about how to use a small-group activity format to develop the lesson and prompt students' engagement and understanding? Small-group activity is highly effective when each member of the group has a role (e.g., recorder, timekeeper, reporter, etc.). It is also effective in allowing students with different abilities and language differences to practice their oral language development and social skills with peers. In addition, the higher-achieving students serve as a role model for reading, problem solving, decoding, oral language, etc., for students who are struggling, have disabilities, or are learning English.

Small-group instruction should also adhere to the time limitation of 10–20 minutes depending on the activity taking place. For example, a small group may be reviewing vocabulary words in a game-type scenario, and this may be appropriate for 10 minutes. Whereas another small-group activity may

FIGURE 30 Students Working in Small Groups

be reading a chunk of a text and then answering a set of questions, which may take longer, but no longer than 20 minutes. It is also recommended that a small group require the participation of 4–6 students for effective role allocation, task completion, and active engagement without frustration.

Adding together the whole group mini-lesson and one small group instructional format, we are now using 30–40 minutes of your reading block. At this point in your lesson, have you considered how you will move students into another type of active learning format? The recommended options include guided reading time and independent reading time. Independent reading time can take several forms. Independent reading can be just that, students reading silently to themselves. It can also be reading in pairs where students each have a role, such as those suggested in Chapter 3. Student matches are carefully selected, and each can provide monitoring of reading fluency and accuracy as well as comprehension and summary practice during reading. Student pairs should also be provided with no more than a 20-minute block. In the meantime, the teacher can facilitate pairs by checking in on how accurate they are following their scripts or roles.

FIGURE 31 Independent Reading Time

FIGURE 32 Guided Reading Time

Teachers can also facilitate small groups of students using other practices, like guided reading groups. Guided reading groups are a highly evidenced-based practice that supports Tier 1 (core), 2, or 3 instruction and intervention. Guided reading is widely used across schools in the U.S. Its focus is to work with students who are at similar reading levels based on a universal assessment or a reading test. Because of the nature of guided reading in using homogeneous groups of students, it serves as a differentiated learning delivery format in any classroom and supports struggling learners, students with disabilities, and English learners.

The goal of guided reading is to serve as a practice stage *after* teacher modeling and *before* independent practice. The guided reading lesson, which lasts between 10–15 minutes, has three main parts at the students' instructional level: before reading strategies, during reading strategies, and after reading strategies (Fountas and Pinnell, 2011). Within each of these areas, each item in Figure 33 is addressed so students can practice with the guidance of a teacher. Then they can move more confidently to independent reading.

Before Reading Strategies	During Reading Strategies	After Reading Strategies
Activation of prior knowledge	Identifying connections to personal experiences	Checking back on predictions and correcting based on text
Building knowledge	Asking questions	Going back to find supporting evidence from text
Setting a purpose for reading	Discussing answers	Analyzing
Using graphic organizers	Making inferences	Checking for understanding using different modalities, like oral response, demonstration response, visual display, etc.
Picture walk or book cover discussion	Teaching strategies for re-reading	
Introduce and review vocabulary	Skimming	
Making predictions	Finding main ideas	Constructing a new ending or extending knowledge
	Finding supporting details	
	Using highlighters or taking notes	Synthesizing points of view

FIGURE 33 Guided Reading Lesson

Guided reading moves students from general knowledge that is usually evident in lower-order thinking skills to higher-order critical thinking skills.

Bloom's Taxonomy

The teacher ensures that all critical thinking skills are addressed based on the students' instructional level by providing ample opportunities for checking for understanding as students read and work on comprehension. Higher-order thinking skills are critical for developing comprehension skills in all students and are a viable means to maintain student engagement by providing a variety of ways to represent their knowledge despite struggles or disabilities. It is important that when delivering the lesson and small-group instruction, teachers carefully plan the questions and activities ahead of time to meet all areas of critical thinking skills.

From many classroom observations, we have seen that teachers typically stay within the constraints of knowledge-based lower-critical

What Are Lower-Order Thinking Skills?

Based on Bloom's Taxonomy, lower-order thinking skills will show that a student can recite information, facts, and dates, and organize the information to solve problems by applying basic concepts to reach solutions.

What Are Higher-Order Thinking Skills?

Higher-order thinking skills involve analysis, synthesis, and evaluation. Students exhibiting higher-order thinking skills will categorize or classify information and compare and contrast it in order to make a decision. Critical thinking draws on (a) skills to generate information (lower-order thinking) and (b) using those skills to guide behavior (higher-order thinking). (Ennis, 1993).

thinking questioning or summarizing skills. Bloom's Taxonomy (1956) or its revised version written by Lorin Anderson, a former student of Bloom (Anderson, Krathwohl, Airasian, Cruikshank, Mayer, Pintrich, Raths, Wittrock, 2000), provides highly structured activities and questioning within each of the six levels from low to high critical thinking skills. Figure 34 shows how students develop thinking skills based on Bloom's Taxonomy and Anderson. The main difference between both is not the levels but the change from nouns to verbs for ease in instructional lesson planning.

Bloom's Levels of Low to High Development Critical Thinking Skills	Anderson's Levels of Low to High Development Critical Thinking Skills
Knowledge	Remembering
Comprehension	Understanding
Application	Applying
Analysis	Analyzing
Synthesis	Evaluating
Evaluation	Creating

FIGURE 34 Comparison of Bloom and Anderson

We recommend that you consider this progression of actions and questioning. Consider how your instruction supports students moving from lower-ordering thinking skills to higher-order thinking skills at their instructional level using a variety of materials, including hi-lo books and grade-level content. It is critical to understand that in each lesson, teachers should teach using all levels and not limit any student or activity to one in particular. Students need practice and role modeling in getting from understanding or summarizing to synthesizing and creating during the learning process.

Literacy Planning

As you can see, if you are able to provide a rich Tier 1 (core) instruction lesson, each student should be actively engaged in learning based on a universal design and appropriate teaching delivery methods. The key in this next set of questions relates planning, based on what we know about attention and engagement of students and how we can deliver the skills, objectives, and standards that they need. Figure 35 illustrates a checklist that may help to monitor your practices in this domain.

In each box, note the *number of activities* the students do to apply and practice literacy skills during independent work time.

Days of Week/Literacy Skill	Monday	Tuesday	Wednesday	Thursday	Friday	Daily Average
Large-group instruction						
Small-group instruction (guided by teacher)						
Small group (peer-mediated mixed-level grouping)						
Small group (same level)						
Pairs (same level)						
Pairs (mixed levels)						
Listening/Technology Center						

FIGURE 35 Literacy Planning Checklist

As you begin to learn and monitor your own progress in delivering a more balanced and active Tier 1 (core) instruction, you will feel more accomplished. Your students are receiving high-quality instruction. In Chapter 2, we talked about how to start implementing different types of activities and small-group instruction in your classroom. Remember that you may be new at this and should only add one additional instructional format until you feel comfortable before adding another. The goal is to have active learning in your classroom every day. Our motto is one change at a time, one teaching practice at a time, one strategy at a time.

Monitoring or tracking your instructional practice works the same way. Track one aspect of your teaching at a time or one chart at a time. Tracking or monitoring using the worksheets we have given you in Figures 28 and 35 serves as a baseline of where you are and where you want to go. Perhaps you discover that you spend 40 minutes in the mini-lesson. So the first change you will do is limit your mini-lesson using a timer or have a student time you. Once you meet that goal, then you can move on to the next skill you decide to adopt in your classroom.

If you already do many of these types of activities, the question is, are they done regularly? Do they address each area of reading? Do students actively partake in monitoring their own learning? Did you bring the students back at the end of the lesson to review the content and evaluate how well they understood? Did you take time to think about what went well in the lesson and what did not?

Self-Monitoring

These last sets of questions address the part of the lesson that we do not usually get to, checking for understanding or evaluation. It is hard! Once your lesson begins, time goes fast. There never seems to be time to evaluate for understanding. However, knowing how many students accessed your instruction and met the standard and objective for the day or week is key. Many schools have students take part in standards-based testing. Standards-based testing is a type of test that mirrors state standardized tests that tell you which standards you are teaching or not. This test helps, but your own daily check for understanding can give you that information as well.

The key is to monitor whether the instruction met the needs of 75%–85% of students in your class. If not, you need to re-teach the objective and standard. We expect that struggling learners, students with disabilities, and English learners may need more exposure or a "second dose," but most of your students should get it in your first try. This also helps you plan for the students who need Tier 2 and perhaps even Tier 3 intervention. It also helps you to pinpoint the reading skill area and standards to be addressed in that intervention. If your testing does not indicate that you are reaching most of your students with your instruction, then you should reflect on what additional or specific areas of your lessons may not be providing a high-quality instruction for your students.

Consider the time you spend teaching in the different reading areas. Is everyone in your small groups following through on their roles? Perhaps you have a challenge with classroom management. These are some things to ponder, but now you can begin to see where you may need help. Reflective practice after each lesson will help you keep abreast of where you need to go. Data from the forms we provided may further help you assess whether you are delivering high-quality instruction.

Conclusion

In this chapter, we provided ways to monitor your own high-quality Tier 1 (core) instruction to ensure that it is differentiated, engaging, balanced, and meets the needs of most students in your classroom. We presented you with a list of questions to determine your lesson's effectiveness and quality. We suggested that without reflecting on your lesson's objective, you cannot adequately assess the specific progress of each student.

In Chapter 1, we introduced you to the MTSS framework and its components, and we described how it works in concert with other initiatives to improve teaching and learning. In Chapter 2, we explained how to use different types of data to learn about your students and how that data can help you develop an instructional approach that is effective and engaging. In Chapter 3, we introduced and explained six reading strategies that you can use today to begin to improve your students' reading skills. And in Chapter 4, we examined individual case studies of students and looked at what type of progress makes sense over time.

We hope that we have provided you with questions and answers to guide your instructional planning and intervention processes and described how hi-lo books can be used to support students' learning. As the country's population changes, schools look very different across urban, suburban, and rural settings with highly divergent factors including race, ethnicity, language, disability, and socio-economic status. Learning about each of the students in your class and what assets they bring (e.g., bilingualism, biculturalism, etc.) is very important as you begin to plan for culturally responsive instruction and intervention supports. Using the same lesson plans year after year does not meet the needs of today's classrooms.

Looking at your classroom through the lens of tiered instruction makes sense and is very effective in organizing support early on. Using educational data to identify your students' strengths and weaknesses and to plan appropriate instruction is what this book is all about. We hope you have learned how to plan for tiered instruction, how to pinpoint your students' basic reading skills the minute they walk into your classroom, and how to continuously monitor their progress from the beginning to the end of the year so that you know when to use targeted curriculum materials and strategies that support reading outcomes.

References

Anderson, L. W., Krathwohl, D. R., Airasian, P. W., Cruikshank, K. A., Mayer, R. E., Pintrich, P. R., Raths, J., Wittrock, M. C. (2000). *A taxonomy for learning, teaching, and assessing: A revision of Bloom's taxonomy of educational objectives.* New York: Pearson, Allyn & Bacon.

August, D. and Shanahan, T. (eds.) (2006). *Developing reading and writing in second-language learners:Lessons from the National Literacy Panel on language-minority children and youth.* Mahwah, NJ: Lawrence Erlbaum Associates.

Batsche, G., Elliot, J., Graden, J. L., Grimes, J., Kovaleski, J. F., & Prasse, D. (2005). *Response to intervention: Policy recommendations and implementation.* Alexandria, VA: National Association of State Directors of Special Education.

Bloom B. S. (1956). *Taxonomy of educational objectives, handbook 1: The cognitive domain.* New York: David McKay Company Inc.

Burns, M. K., Riley-Tillman, T. C., & VanDerHeyden, A. M. (2012). *RTI applications, Volume 1: Academic and behavioral interventions.* New York: The Guilford Press.

Colvin, G., & Lazar, M. (1997). *The effective elementary classroom: Managing for success.* Longmont, CO: Sopris West.

Colvin, G., Sugai, G., & Patching, W. (1993). Pre-correction: An instructional strategy for managing predictable behavior problems. *Intervention in School and Clinic, 28,* 143–150.

Dalton, J. Smith, D. (1986). *Extending children's special abilities: Strategies for the primary classroom.* Retrieved from http://www.icc.edu/innovation/PDFS/assessmentevaluation/revisedBloomschart_bloomsverbsmatrix.pdf

Darch, C. B., & Kameenui, E. J. (2003). *Instructional classroom management: A proactive approach to behavior management.* (2nd ed.). White Plains, NY: Longman.

Fountas, I. C., & Pinnell, G. S. (1996). *Guided reading: Good first teaching for all children.* Portsmouth, NH: Heinemann.

Fountas, I. C., & Pinnell, G. S. (2012). Guided reading: The romance and the reality. *The Reading Teacher, 66*(4), 268–284.

Frayer, D. Frederick, W. C., and Klausmejer, H. J. (1969). *A schema for testing the level of cognitive mastery.* Madison, WI: Wisconsin Center for Educational Research.

Fuchs, D., Fuchs, L. S., Mathes, P. G., & Simmons, D. C. (1997). Peer-assisted learning strategies: Making classrooms more responsive to diversity. *American Educational Research Journal, 34*(1), 174–206.

Gay, G., & Howard, T. C. (2000). Multicultural teacher education for the 21st century. *The Teacher Educator, 36*(1), 1–16.

Hall, T. (2002). *Differentiated instruction.* Wakefield, MA: National Center on Accessing the General Curriculum.

Hasbrouck, J. & Tindal, G. A. (2006). Oral reading fluency norms: A valuable assessment tool for reading teachers. *The Reading Teacher, 59*(7), 636–644.

Hernandez, D. J. (2011). *Double jeopardy: How third-grade reading skills and poverty influence high school graduation.* Baltimore, MD: The Annie E. Casey Foundation.

The IRIS Center for Training Enhancements. (2008). *CSR: A reading comprehension strategy.* Retrieved from http://iris.peabody.vanderbilt.edu/module/csr/

The IRIS Center for Training Enhancements. (2012). *Secondary reading instruction: Teaching vocabulary and comprehension in the content areas.* Retrieved from http://iris.peabody.vanderbilt.edu/module/sec-rdng/

Jones, V. F. & Jones, L. S. (2001). *Comprehensive classroom management: Creating communities of support and solving problems* (6th ed.). Boston: Allyn & Bacon.

Kameenui, E. J., & Carnine, D. W. (2002). *Effective teaching strategies that accommodate diverse learners* (2nd ed.). Upper Saddle River, NJ: Merrill.

Klingner, J. K., & Vaughn, S. (1998). Using collaborative strategic reading. *Teaching Exceptional Children, 30*(6), 32–37.

Latham, G. I. (1997). *Behind the schoolhouse door: Eight skills every teacher should have.* Utah State University, Logan. Mountain Plains Regional Resource Center.

Latham, G. (1992). Interacting with at-risk children: The positive position. *Principal, 72*(1), 26–30.

Lesaux, N. (2013). *PreK–3rd: Getting literacy instruction right.* New York, NY: Foundation for Child Development.

Marston, D. (2005). Tiers of intervention in responsiveness to intervention: Prevention outcomes and learning disabilities identification patterns. *Journal of Learning Disabilities, 38,* 539–544.

Martella, R. C., Nelson, J. R., & Marchand-Martella, N. E. (2003). *Managing disruptive behaviors in the schools: A schoolwide, classroom, and individualized social learning approach.* Boston, MA: Allyn & Bacon.

National Education Association. (2014). Retrieved from http://www.nea.org/

Paine, S. C., Radicchi, J., Rosellini, L. C., Deutchman, L., & Darch, C. B. (1983). *Structuring your classroom for academic success.* Champaign, IL: Research Press.

Pavri, S. (2010). Response to intervention in the social-emotional-behavioral domain: Perspectives from urban schools. *Teaching Exceptional Children Plus, 6*(3). 2–11.

Petersen-Brown, S., & Burns, M. K. (2011). Adding a vocabulary component to incremental rehearsal to enhance retention and generalization. *School Psychology Quarterly, 26*(3), 245.

Reading Rockets: Launching Young Readers. (2014). Retrieved from http://www.readingrockets.org/

Rinaldi, C., Higgins Averill, O., & Stuart, S. (2011). Response to intervention: Educators' perceptions of a three-year RTI reform effort in an urban elementary school. *Journal of Education, 191*(2), 43–53.

RTI Action Network. (2014). Retrieved from http://www.rtinetwork.org/

Spectrum K12 School Solutions. (2011). *Response to intervention adoption survey 2011.* Retrieved from http://www.spectrumk12 .com//uploads/file/RTI%20Report%202011%20FINAL.pdf

White, S. & Clement, J. (2001). *Assessing the Lexile Framework: Results of a panel meeting, NCES 2001–08.* Washington, DC: U.S. Department of Education, National Center for Education Statistics.

Appendix

- "Getting to Know You" Information Form
- "Reading Instruction" Teacher Self-Assessment
- Teacher Action Planning
- "Partner Reading" Correction Card
- "Shrink It!" Correction Card
- "Collaborative Strategic Reading" Role Cue Cards
- "Collaborative Strategic Reading" Clunk Cards
- Sample "Collaborative Strategic Reading" Learning Log
- "Collaborative Strategic Reading" Learning Log
- Common Planning Time: Asking Questions of Your Data
- "The Frayer Method" Graphic Organizer
- Fidelity Checklist
- Literacy Planning Checklist

"Getting to Know You" Information Form

NAME: _____ DATE: _____

Directions: All about you! Fill out the form. Write as much about yourself as you can.

[drawing box] Draw a picture of yourself or something that represents who you are.	What language other than English do you speak? _____ What language would you like to learn to speak? _____ What is your favorite thing to do after school? _____ _____ _____ _____
What do you like best about school? _____	Do you have siblings? Younger or older? _____
If you could change one thing about school, what would it be? _____ _____ _____ _____	How do you do your homework? ☐ In silence at a desk ☐ In silence somewhere else ☐ With music at a desk ☐ With music in your room ☐ With many breaks ☐ Quickly, no breaks
What activities in class help you learn best? _____	What is your favorite subject? _____
Describe the things your favorite teacher did when he or she was teaching? _____	What is the most difficult thing you have been asked to do in school? _____
What activities do you like to do in class from most to least, using 1 as the most and 5 the least. _____ Listen to the teacher _____ Engage in class discussion _____ Work in small groups _____ Work in pairs _____ Work on the computer _____ Present your work in front of the class _____ Debate ideas with other students	Check the types of books you are familiar with. ☐ Graphic novels ☐ Classics ☐ E-books ☐ Fiction ☐ Nonfiction

"Reading Instruction" Teacher Self-Assessment

The purpose of this self-assessment is to provide you with elements of high-quality Tier 1 (core) instruction indicators. The instrument should be used 3 times per year to ensure fidelity of your lesson planning and delivery. At each complete, please fill in the Teacher Action Planning form on page 113.

Directions: Using a scale of 0–4, please rate yourself.

- Not in Place = 0
- Partially in Place (1%–25% of the time) = 1
- In Place (25%–75% of the time) = 2
- Achieved (75%–95% of the time) = 3
- Sustaining (95%–100% of the time) = 4

NAME: _____ DATE: _____

Lesson and Instructional Indicators	0	1	2	3	4
1. Goals and academic objectives are posted in the classroom.					
2. Goals and behavioral objectives are posted in the classroom.					
3. Goals and academic objectives are presented to the students.					
4. Goals and behavioral objectives are presented to the students.					
5. Teacher engages students in activation of prior knowledge and uses students' backgrounds, experiences, culture, and language to link the instructional concept.					

Table continued on p. 112

Lesson and Instructional Indicators	0	1	2	3	4
6. Teacher introduces new concepts as a whole-group activity using UDL principles and explicit instruction on reading priorities. • Addresses word attack strategies (phonemic awareness, phonics, and decoding) • Provides fluency practice (independent and guides with strategy instruction) • Engages in comprehension questions from low-critical thinking to high-critical thinking skills • Explicitly teaches and engages students in vocabulary instruction and use					
7. Teacher provides guided reading opportunities and practice of the new concepts orally and in writing. • As a whole group • Peer-mediated activities					
8. Teacher provides summaries of the concept learned.					
9. Teacher evaluates students' understanding of the lesson. • Exit slip check • Written assignment • Oral assignment • Quizzes • Other					
10. Teacher reflects on the lesson and reviews which aspects were delivered as intended.					
11. Teacher collects progress-monitoring check-ups on all students 3 times per year.					
12. Teacher collects and evaluates progress of students receiving intervention supports.					
13. Teacher problem-solves with colleagues to ensure that high-quality core instruction is being delivered across the grades.					

Teacher Action Planning

Time Frame	Focus	Evidence/Data
September to January	I will _____. _____ _____ _____ _____ _____	
February to June	I have _____. _____ _____ _____ _____ And I will _____. _____ _____ _____ _____	
Summary	This year I _____. _____ _____ _____ _____	

Partner Reading Correction Card

Partner 2 reads a word incorrectly, skips a word, or does not say a word within 4 seconds.

Partner 1 says, "Check it!"

Partner 1 says, "What is this word?"

Partner 2 says, "I need some help."

Partner 1 says, "That word is _____. What word?"

Partner 2 repeats the word

Partner 1 says, "Good. Please read the sentence again."

Partner 2 re-reads the sentence

OR

Partner 1 says, "Check it!"

Partner 1 says, "What is this word?"

Partner 2 says the word correctly

Partner 1 says, "Good. Please read the sentence again."

Partner 2 re-reads the sentence

Shrink It! Correction Card

If Partner 2 gives the wrong answer, Partner 1 will say, "Try again!"

Partner 2 tries to answer again.

If Partner 2 gives another wrong answer, Partner 1 will say, "Here's a hint." (Provide a hint.)

If Partner 2 still cannot answer correctly, Partner 1 will say, "The answer is _____." (Give the answer.)

OR

If Partner 2 says the main idea in more than 10 words, Partner 1 says, "Shrink it!"

"Collaborative Strategic Reading" Role Cue Cards

Gist Expert Cue Card

1. "What is the most important idea we have learned about the topic so far? Everyone think of the gist and write it in your learning log."

2. "Announcer, please call on someone to share their gist."

3. "Does anyone have a different gist they would like to share?"

4. Announcer, call on someone else to share their gist."

5. Help your group come up with a gist that includes the most important information, leaves out details, and is ten words or less.

The IRIS Center for Training Enhancements. (2008). *CSR: A reading comprehension strategy.* Retrieved from http://iris.peabody.vanderbilt.edu/module/csr/

"Collaborative Strategic Reading" Role Cue Cards

Leader Cue Card #1

Before Reading

1. "We know that today's topic is
   —————."

2. "Let's brainstorm and write in our learning logs everything we already know about the topic."

3. "Who would like to share their best ideas?"

4. "Now let's predict. Look at the title, pictures, and headings and think about what we might learn today. Write your ideas in your learning logs."

Leader Cue Card #2

During Reading

1. "Who would like to read the section?"

2. Click and Clunk – "Did everyone understand what we read? If you did not, write your clunks in your learning log."

3. If someone has a clunk – "Clunk Expert, please help us out."

4. Get the Gist – "It's time to Get the Gist. Gist Expert, please help us out."

5. Repeat the steps on this card again for each section read.

Leader Cue Card #3

After Reading

1. "Now let's think of some questions to check if we really understood what we read."

   "Remember to start your questions with **who, what, where, when, why, or how**. Everyone write your questions in your learning log."

2. "Who would like to share their best question?"

3. "In our learning logs, let's write down as much as we can about what we learned."

4. "Let's go around the group and each share something we learned."

Leader Cue Card #4

After Reading

Compliments and Suggestions

1. "The Encourager has been watching carefully and will now tell us two things we did really well as a group today."

2. "Is there anything that would help us do even better next time?"

The IRIS Center for Training Enhancements. (2008). *CSR: A reading comprehension strategy.*
Retrieved from http://iris.peabody.vanderbilt.edu/module/csr/

"Collaborative Strategic Reading" Role Cue Cards

Clunk Expert Cue Card

1. "What is your clunk?"
2. "Does anyone know the meaning of the clunk?"

If YES

a. "Please explain what the clunk means."
b. "Does everyone understand now?"

If NO

a. Read Clunk Card #1.

The IRIS Center for Training Enhancements. (2008). *CSR: A reading comprehension strategy.* Retrieved from http://iris.peabody.vanderbilt.edu/module/csr/

"Collaborative Strategic Reading" Role Cue Cards

Announcer Cue Card #1

Before Reading

1. Call on at least two people to say what they know.
2. Call on at least two people to say what they think they will learn.
3. Call on different people to read.

Remember to make sure only one person talks at a time!

Announcer Cue Card #2

During Reading

1. *Clunks* – Call on students who have clunks.
2. Call on students to help fix clunks.
3. Gists – Call on one person to say the gist.
4. Call on at least one other person to say his or her version of the gist.

Announcer Cue Card #3

After Reading

1. Call on two students to share their best questions.
2. Call on students to answer the questions.
3. Call on all students to say something they learned.

The IRIS Center for Training Enhancements. (2008). *CSR: A reading comprehension strategy.* Retrieved from http://iris.peabody.vanderbilt.edu/module/csr/

"Collaborative Strategic Reading" Role Cue Cards

Encourager Cue Card #1

Before Reading

1. Brainstom – Tell Someone they did a good job saying what they already know.
2. Predict – Tell someone they did a good job saying what they think they will learn.

Encourager Cue Card #2

During Reading

1. Click and Clunk – Tell someone they did a good job figuring out a clunk.
2. Get the Gist – Tell someone they did a good job getting the gist.

Encourager Cue Card #3

After Reading

1. Wrap-up questions – Tell someone they asked a good question.
2. Wrap-up review – Tell someone they did a good job saying what they learned.

Encourager Cue Card #4

After Reading

1. Tell two things your group did well today.
2. Tell two things your group can do even better next time.

The IRIS Center for Training Enhancements. (2008). *CSR: A reading comprehension strategy.*
Retrieved from http://iris.peabody.vanderbilt.edu/module/csr/

"Collaborative Strategic Reading" Clunk Cards

Clunk Card #1

Re-read the sentence with the clunk and look for key ideas to help you figure out the word. Think about what makes sense.

"Can anyone now explain the meaning of the clunk?"

If **NO**, go to Clunk Card #2

Clunk Card #2

Re-read the sentences before and after the clunk looking for clues.

"Can anyone **now** explain the meaning of the clunk?"

If **NO**, go to Clunk Card #3

Clunk Card #3

Look for a prefix or suffix in the word that might help.

"Can anyone **now** explain the meaning of the clunk?"

If **NO**, go to Clunk Card #4

Clunk Card #4

Break the word apart and look for smaller words that you know.

"Can anyone **now** explain the meaning of the clunk?"

If **NO**, ask the teacher for help.

The IRIS Center for Training Enhancements. (2008). *CSR: A reading comprehension strategy.* Retrieved from http://iris.peabody.vanderbilt.edu/module/csr/

Sample "Collaborative Strategic Reading" Learning Log

CSR Learning Log

Topic: _Ecosystems_   Date: _03/10/XX_

1. What I already know about the topic:

   An ecosystem is the environment.

2. What I think I will learn:

   I will learn something about deserts and rain forests.

Clunks:	Clunks:	Clunks:
harmony – in peace with each other	interdependence – relying on each other	
Gist:	Gist:	Gist:
The parts of an ecosystem rely on each other.	An ecosystem can be broken.	

Questions about the important ideas in the passage:

What is an ecosystem?
What happens if a part of an ecosystem is damaged?

What I learned:

The ecosystems need to be taken care of.

The IRIS Center for Training Enhancements. (2008). *CSR: A reading comprehension strategy.* Retrieved from http://iris.peabody.vanderbilt.edu/module/csr/

"Collaborative Strategic Reading" Learning Log

CSR Learning Log

Topic: _____

Date: _____

1. What I already know about the topic:

2. What I think I will learn:

Clunks:

Gist:

Clunks:

Gist:

Clunks:

Gist:

Questions about the important ideas in the passage:

What I learned:

The IRIS Center for Training Enhancements. (2008). *CSR: A reading comprehension strategy.*
Retrieved from http://iris.peabody.vanderbilt.edu/module/csr/

Common Planning Time: Asking Questions of Your Data

What data do you look at to find out how many students are succeeding in their reading comprehension?

Use the following questions to engage in a data-informed discussion of instructional planning. One teacher should act as a facilitator and ensure that all members of the team have an opportunity to reflect on their data.

- Which students grew the most? Why do you think that is?
- What instructional strategies (e.g., peer-assisted learning) did you use to teach the skill that had the most gains?
- Which students grew the least? Why do you think that is?
- What barriers to learning might have affected the way you taught the skill that had the least gains?
- What do you need to do to improve your instruction of low-scoring skills (e.g., time, access to materials, more training)?
- What type of formative assessments do you use to measure growth (daily quiz, exit ticket, etc.)?
- What affected the fidelity of your implementation of instruction and interventions (e.g., time, absences, lack of training)?
- How can you improve fidelity of implementation in the future?
- How can you use this data to support your professional learning goals and activities?

"The Frayer Method" Graphic Organizer

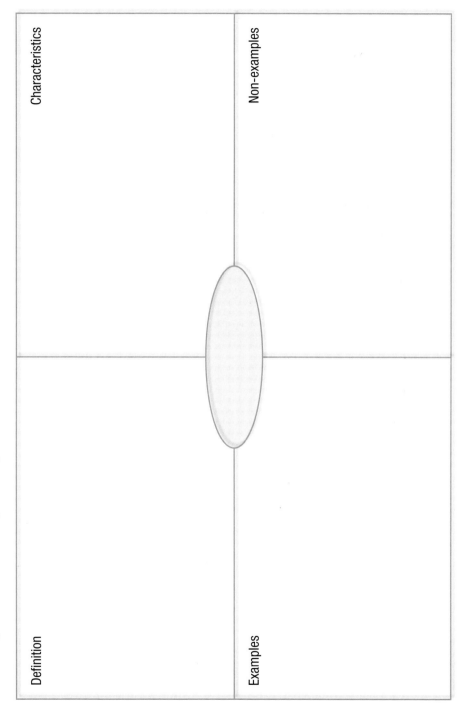

Definition

Characteristics

Examples

Non-examples

Fidelity Checklist

Literacy Skills

Phonemic Awareness: identifying sounds (phonemes) in spoken words

Word Attack: decoding words in connected text, linking the ability to read isolated sounds to new words

Fluency: reading a text quickly and with accuracy

Vocabulary: understanding words to get meaning and to convey meaning

Comprehension: understanding the meaning of a text in connected text

In each box, note the *number of minutes* you teach the above literacy skills to your whole group.

Days of Week/ Reading Skill	Monday	Tuesday	Wednesday	Thursday	Friday	Daily Average
Phonemic Awareness						
Word Attack						
Fluency						
Vocabulary						
Comprehension						

Literacy Planning Checklist

In each box, note the *number of activities* the students do to apply and practice literacy skills during independent work time.

Days of Week/Literacy Skill	Monday	Tuesday	Wednesday	Thursday	Friday	Daily Average
Large-group instruction						
Small-group instruction (guided by teacher)						
Peer-mediated small group (mixed levels)						
Small group (same level)						
Pairs (same level)						
Pairs (mixed levels)						
Listening/Technology Center						